# A Non-Violent Lifestyle

# A Non-Violent Lifestyle

*Conversations with Jean and Hildegard Goss*

by Gérard Houver

translated by
Richard Bateman

LAMP

Marshall Morgan and Scott
Lamp Press
34–42 Cleveland Street, London, W1P 5FB. U.K.

Copyright © 1981 Hildegard and Jean Goss-Mayr
First published 1981 in France by Les Éditions du Cerf
under the title *Jean et Hildegarde Goss, La non-violence, c'est
la vie*
First published in the UK in 1989 by Marshall Morgan and
Scott Publications Ltd
Part of the Marshall Pickering Holdings Group

*British Library Cataloguing in Publication Data*
Houver, G.
  A non-violent lifestyle.
  1. Peace – Christian viewpoints
  I. Title
  261.8′73

ISBN: 0–551–01770–8




Text Set in Linotron Sabon
Phototypeset by Input Typesetting Ltd, London
Printed in Great Britain by
Courier International Ltd, Tiptree, Essex

# *Foreword*

My meeting with Hildegard and Jean Goss and their friendship have greatly enriched both myself and my work. The publication of this book in an invitation to the reader to get to know these two apostles of non-violent love.

It is also a warning to the reader: a careful and sympathetic reading can bring him to a point of crisis and lead him to take a radical decision which will overturn all his relationships and his whole life.

I have known Hildegard Mayr for nearly thirty years. After she had read the first German edition of my book *The Law of Christ*, Hildegard discerned in me a future apostle of non-violence and, in that hope, came to see me. I must confess that at that time I had some reservations about the somewhat fanatical side of complete non-violence. I believed at the most in a non-violence which would arise out of a reduction to the minimum of violence in the individual sphere as much as in society.

Hildegard was very direct and very frank in expounding her point of view. She did not persuade me of the absolute character of non-violence, but she made a great impression on me by her personality, her truly non-violent character.

In other words, without even talking about it, Hildegard persuaded me by her charisma, by her vocation, to promulgate the spirituality of the *satyagraha*, of non-violence. It was the witness of her transparent faith which compelled me to listen to her message.

Shortly after her marriage I got to know her husband Jean and I could not help loving his unreserved devotion to the Gospel of Love which knows how to conquer violence, hatred, bitterness.

Jean's character is quite different than that of Hildegard,

so that the one completes the other: in fact they represent the archetype of complimentary personalities.

I think that Jean could well have become a revolutionary, in the traditional and powerful sense of the word; he is not lacking in what one might call 'psychological aggression'. But, thank God, Jean did not choose violence, without going so far as to renounce or destroy his natural aggression which he was able to channel into a love both serene and aggressive.

When one knows Jean, one realizes the failings of the theory of Konrad Lorenz, according to which man is, in some measure, condemned to a violent and dangerous aggression.

Jean and Hildegard have not renounced human passion, but they have directed all their energies, all their passions, all their intelligence, their actions and their initiative towards a life which is the incarnation of the 'power of truth' (*satyagraha*, as Gandhi called it) and which proclaims that the way of non-violent and courageous love is the only solution to the problem of violence, which has become an apocalyptic one for our generation.

Hildegard and Jean are undoubtedly attractive prophets, but not comfortable ones.

It is precisely through the total sincerity of their witness and the simplicity of their faith, that the Gospel comes alive; but it is a source of disturbance to all those who would be Christians whilst leading a life of tranquility.

For the last thirty years Hildegard and Jean have led a quite 'impossible' life: they have been to the very limits of exhaustion, risk, zeal and even torture. Their urgent need to evangelize is like that of St Paul. Like him they are completely captive to their vocation to spread the Gospel: the whole Gospel, not just a few tactics or strategies of non-violence. They are, so to speak, the key, the pivot of a profound vision, of an active and creative spirituality of non-violence. Like Paul, they feel that 'time is short.' They sense this in a new way: it is vital that men shake off ideologies and the shackles of violence, of armaments and of war.

vi

Anyone who realizes that in this book there is an authentic alternative (conversion to the Gospel, to non-violent love, to creative liberty, which allow for non-violent defence of the people) cannot help but become its apostle.

Jean and Hildegard believe that we can be changed to the roots of our beings and that once transformed ('made conscious') we can bring about a radical turning-point of history, before nuclear deterrence becomes the total destruction of mankind.

What I admire most is that Hildegard and Jean have never grown discouraged, despite the numerous difficulties which they have encountered, even amongst Christians. This faithfulness to their prophetic mission, this serenity, can only be explained by their faith in Grace, in the power of Grace and by their trust in the inner resources of man redeemed by Christ. They do not feel themselves to be dependent on immediate success but seek the desired result with all their might: that is the spiritual success which goes hand in hand with the strategy of non-violence.

The person who, like them, sees for himself the failure of all this fine talk of mutually controlled disarmament and the increase of even more catastrophic threats, may not waste the precious time which we still have. I am convinced that there is only one solution: that of creative non-violence. We are in urgent need of it, not only to overcome the terror of the strategy of deterrence which, with its armory, could destroy all life on our planet, but also to be this new creation of man and of the world which our Saviour offers us.

Gérard Houver, who brings us his conversation with Hildegard and Jean, those 'flaming arrows,' this creative and intelligent witness, is a convert of Jean. He swears that their meeting transformed his life and that of his family and that he owes him his gratitude and his happiness.

Anyone who reads these pages must also be ready to be swept off his feet with unimaginable consequences for himself and those around him. Perhaps also there will be someone who reads this book out of mere curiosity, having at the outset a thousand objections ready to hand . . . and yet, it may be that he too will discover how genuine are both the message and those who bear it.

Fr. Bernard Häring

Foreword translated from the French by Jean and John Andrews

# I

**JEAN.** — Now get this straight: at first I spoke of love, of the power of love, and everybody agreed with me. There was no problem there, they all knew about love: it's in all novels and sermons. But everybody continued to approve of butcheries, or even carry them out.

Then I changed. I explained to my listeners that they had to believe in the truth and act according to the truth. Once again I was met with total, placid agreement. That's understandable, since nobody wants to admit to being a liar.

I looked for something else: justice. I spoke of the power of justice, of commitment to the service of justice. I was greeted with unanimous agreement. Justice had to be re-established, and everyone found an injustice of which he or she had been a victim, but they very rarely felt concerned by injustices they themselves had committed.

And then I found the word: non-violence. I said 'no' to violence. Everybody was up in arms.

It's not that I set out to confuse my listeners just for the pleasure of it, but to say 'no' you must raise your head, you must show yourself, you must be a man and not a slave. By saying non-violence, I begin by refusing a fatality: of violence, that is, of evil. The evil in me, the evil around me is not inevitable.

When I say 'no' to violence, I act as a free man, I give man all his human dimension, and, in addition, I give him his divine dimension.

**GÉRARD.** — Officials talk about human dignity, liberty, even the divine dimension, and they never, never provoke indignation. On the contrary, they are applauded, feebly, it's true, because they are trotting out the same old story. But you only have to pronounce the word 'non-violence' to let passions loose. Why is that? It can't just be a question of vocabulary.

**JEAN.** — A man comes along. He says the only thing of real value in the world is man; that nothing, absolutely nothing, allows you to kill him or be disrespectful to him. He says we owe love to every man, be he the worst of criminals or your mortal enemy. What happened to this man? Was he called a utopian, an idealist, a dreamer? No! He was killed because he was a very dangerous individual. Have you ever heard of a country where they lock up people who just want to dream of a better world in a corner of their own room?

Dreamers aren't dangerous. Most advocates of non-violence have done time in prisons, in camps, and almost all the great non-violent people have been assassinated, like Jesus. That's no accident.

There's certainly a problem of vocabulary: many people confuse aggressivity with violence, and non-violence with a sort of 'castration'. The non-violent person would be a mollusc, some flabby sort of animal who stands up against nothing, neither other people nor events, who lets others do as they wish and do with him as they wish. Well it's not like that at all! All non-violent people are aggressive. They attack other people in their consciences, they are extremely aggressive towards evil and injustice. A man who doesn't stand up against injustice isn't a man. Gandhi said you could do nothing with a coward, but from a violent man you could make a non-violent one. If I slap your face and you are normal, you react, you don't let me get away with it. . . .

**GÉRARD.** — Let's talk about that slap, it has a long history! Since Jesus said that we should turn the other cheek, it has been everybody's laughing-stock; besides, when it actually happened to him — during the trial —

2

he didn't turn the other cheek either, as far as I can remember.

**JEAN.** — That's true, he didn't let them get away with it. He attacked his torturer: 'Why do you strike me?' If he had been like me, he would have kept quiet; if you speak you run the risk of another blow, or worse. And if he had spat in his torturer's face, what would have happened to him? All the same it is strange: there was no second slap. Only the strongest are capable of turning the other cheek. It stops the massacre. It goes even further: it doesn't allow the other person to call himself a brute. I was a prisoner in Germany during the last war. We had a guard who had come back from the Russian front, and who had fits of raving madness. During these fits he got carried away and started beating up the prisoners. One of them had the courage to go to him and say: 'I'm volunteering. If you need to maltreat someone, hit me.' The torturer couldn't believe his ears: 'How many blows do you want?' 'I'll leave that to your conscience,' answered the prisoner. That was the last straw, the thing you shouldn't say. Conscience — 'I'm a brute, an instrument, I'm not a conscience. I have no conscience — I haven't got the right to have a conscience.' It took him some time to realize the opposite, but the floggings were finished.

Besides, when someone hits you, do you return it straight away? No. You begin by looking at the build of the man who hit you, you judge his weight, and only then do you react.

The first reflex is, naturally, to demolish the aggressor, to kill him; it's not a question of reason, it's instinctive. When it comes to judging, you've already taken the first step towards humanization: turning the other cheek or its equivalent is truly the gesture of a free man, so a typically non-violent gesture.

**GÉRARD.** — The examples you quote are valid individually, but how easy is it to transpose them onto another level?

3

**HILDEGARD.** — The first time we went to live in Latin America, in 1962, we found such a 'revolting' situation, that is, so much injustice, that we thought the peasants there had no alternative to killing to put an end to their misery. They had nothing to lose.

They were the ones who taught us about non-violence. To kill effectively you need arms, and arms are never in the hands of the poor, always in the hands of the rich. Everyone knows the rich never give anything for nothing, not even machine-guns. You must always pay.

The *campesinos* (poor peasants) had discovered non-violence out of necessity.

In their struggle they don't want to provoke the violence of the authorities. If they use violence the authorities' violence will always be there to crush them, and it will always be the stronger.

We often forget that to be violent you must have enough to eat. Men who are sick with hunger and who have inherited famine, revolt in order to eat, to have some work, but their revolt is generally pacific. Developing a theory of armed revolution, as Che Guevara and Camillo Torres did in their time, is the privilege of the rich and of intellectuals. They had moved away from the reality of the people.

**JEAN.** — That doesn't diminish their generosity, or the considerable impact their sacrifices and their lives had on the conscience of many men, as much in Latin America as in the rest of the world. Che was a doctor, and Camillo Torres, whom I knew personally, was a priest. He chose violence to 'defend his people', to defend justice, to defend love. He wanted to defend by killing. Killing who? Those who produced injustice, those who encouraged hatred and lies? In reality he would have only killed police and soldiers; in a word, people like himself, as little responsible as he himself was for general injustice.

Can you imagine the Czechs, in 1968, revolting against the Russians with whatever arms they could find? Who would they have killed? Third rank Ivans and Dimitris, while those who were responsible were well out of the way!

We live with some tragic illusions. The first illusion identifies in our mind the man with the evil he does. We almost always draw the conclusion that we only need to kill the man to kill the evil. I say we 'almost always' reason like that, because there is one exception; when you yourself are concerned you never make that identification. The second is of the same sort: we believe we must always defend the great human values: Truth, Justice, Liberty, Love, by all means at our disposal, including killing.

We kill, we make war, for the love of Truth, of Justice, of Liberty. It's not going too far to add this: we kill men for the love of man.

It was a soldier, Colonel Dominique Chavanot, who said: 'If, in the name of humanism, we are led to destroy man, we are doing exactly the opposite of what we intended.'[1] For him this expresses the rejection of torture, but, for me, every injustice, every war, all political or economic exploitation is torture: a negation of man.


**HILDEGARD.** — The outcry against non-violence comes more deeply from our need for security. Not to be violent any more is to let oneself be invaded by the other. The psychologists say we are threatened in our unity, but it's more than that. I can explain better with an example from experience. Everything we call non-violence has one source only, for Jean as for me, only one origin, only one driving force: Love made man, Jesus Christ. The Gospel is our only guide, we have no other. Now, those whose duty it is to teach the Gospel, to continue Christ's and the apostles' teaching, those who call themselves the disciples of Jesus — the churches, the Christians — are very rarely in favour of non-violence. No Christian church is non-violent. Let me explain: no church has had the courage to affirm that, in no circumstances, has one the right to kill a man. They have all found and admitted exceptions in which one could kill; and exceptions are like reels of

5

thread: you begin by pulling a little bit off ... and the whole lot comes with it.

We'll get to the root of the problem, I think. Here, I'm just quoting this example to show how men and women, who are sincerely attached to Christ, to the man who has lived Love, Justice and Truth as no one has ever lived them, take fright when you talk about renouncing violence.

**GÉRARD.** — Violence seems to be the guarantee of our security. Insecurity provokes fear, and fear, violence.

So we are going to proceed in the opposite direction: the more violent I am, the less afraid I am.

But can we live without security? A man has the right to security, a family has the right to security, and that goes for a nation, too. Why should a church, a religion not have the right to security?

**JEAN.** — In 1981, according to the Stockholm International Peace Research Institute (SIPRI), we are going to spend the sum of 600 billion dollars on arms — for our supposed security. The Warsaw Pact and NATO have the capacity to destroy all human life fifty times over. As if once wasn't enough! Not to mention bacteriological and chemical weapons which multiply a hundred-fold the destructive capacity of those powers so worried about our well-being and security.

How many times will we have to be able to destroy mankind in order to feel secure?

But whose security are we talking about? The security of those who are dying of hunger, who haven't got a drop of milk to survive on, who haven't got a square yard of their own to sleep in, the security of people who see their children die because they have nothing to treat them with?

No! We're talking about our own. The security of the well-fed, the satisfied, the educated. On this earth, we haven't even got enough to give a kilo of bread or rice to each inhabitant, but we, the powerful countries, have put aside 20,000 kilos of explosive for every single person,

6

including children and old people. In the year 2000, the total amount of plutonium available in the world will be the equivalent of a million atomic bombs.[2]

Are we mad? We believe, as we are taught, that there are two systems opposed to each other on this planet: it's not true! The economic and political complex in which we live has no nationality, only converging interests which exploit and govern countries of widely differing obediences. That will continue for as long as it takes to discover that man is the unique value in the world, and that we should respect man in the absolute.

**HILDEGARD.** — There are historically pacifist churches, the Mennonite church, for example, but it is true that none of the three major Christian confessions, Catholic, Orthodox and Protestant, affirm the absolute respect for man in all circumstances; and yet they always claim the right to liberty, justice and dignity for themselves when they are oppressed.

But basically I think that religions — that is, Christians, that is all of us, don't want to live in insecurity. The biblical word for insecurity is 'poverty'.

Poverty is the first condition for living non-violence — I mean evangelical poverty, the first of the beatitudes. It influences all the others. The kingdom of heaven is there in the present, not the future.

It isn't by chance that the poor discover non-violence and the Gospel at the same time, as in Latin America. 'Being poor is not interesting: all the poor agree with that. What is interesting is to possess the Kingdom of heaven; but only the poor can do that.'[3]

We put our security into the hands of idols: banks and bombs, instead of putting it into the hands of Love, that is, into the hands of the Lord. 'Some trust in chariots, and some in horses: but we will remember the name of the lord our God. They are brought down and fallen: but we are risen, and stand upright' (Ps 20, 8–9).

**GÉRARD.** — With believers, as with non-believers, you

7

have the same reaction regarding non-violence: strong opposition; and yet, if you question people, nobody admits they are violent — nobody is in favour of violence. It seems as if violence exerts a sort of fascination on us; as Girard says: 'The subject adores violence and hates it.'[4]

I wonder if the aggressivity provoked by non-violence, when we are faced with it, doesn't come from the fact 'that men can not face the senseless nakedness of their own violence without risking giving themselves up to that same violence; they have always ignored it, at least partially, and the possibility of really human societies could well depend on this ignoring'.[5]

**HILDEGARD.** — We are all a bit blind where violence is concerned; we have a sort of fear in ourselves which prevents us from looking violence in the face. When you denounce violence you attack the organization of society. I think the episode in the Gospel of the woman taken in adultery, as John tells it, is typical in this respect: a woman is caught in the act of adultery — alone, of course; the men are only there to denounce her. Mosaïc law is clear on this point: this sin is the equivalent of idolatry. She should be stoned to death; she has broken one of God's commandments. What is Jesus going to do? He is confronted with sacred institutions: divine law, mosaïc law, and the functioning of these laws produce death, that is, absolute violence. The pharisees are in the right; the law, and even morality are on their side. What does Jesus do? He stays silent for a time and bends down. Who stays standing? The pharisees and the woman. Jesus obliges the pharisees to look at the woman, to see her as she is: a woman, and not just a 'case in law'. Then he straightens up and says: 'He that is without sin among you, let him first cast a stone at her.'

Stoning is like a firing squad, or a bombardment: everybody kills, but nobody is a murderer. Jesus doesn't want this anonymity: throw your stone if you are pure, if you think you have the right to kill in the name of 'He who is most pure', of 'He who is without sin', that is, God.

The pharisees are brought face to face with their own violence. Up till then they had got rid of their violence and their sins by transferring them to the woman — in the name of God, in the name of the law. That's the way things still turn out today.

'Men manage to transfer their violence that much more easily when the transfer process appears not to be theirs, but an absolute imperative, an order from a God whose demands are as terrible as they are detailed.'[6]

He writes in the sand again. What? Certainly the truth, perhaps the sins of those around him.

They 'went out one by one, beginning at the eldest', and Jean, my husband, always claims that the last ones ran away.

What did Jesus do? He attacked their consciences with truth, but he didn't stop there — he never stops there: he proves his love to the person he attacks.

Truth without love, justice without love are murderous weapons. Jesus placed each one face to face with his own truth, his own violence; he condemned nobody, since he said: 'Neither do I condemn thee'. He freed the Pharisees from their violence and the woman from hers. He is just right up to the end; he doesn't clear her: 'go,' he says, 'and sin no more.'

With Judas, Jesus has the same attitude; he tells the truth: 'You betray me,' he says, but in a phrase that expresses love at the same time: 'My friend'.

I think the 'violence' that the manifestation of non-violence lets loose is partly the result of this fear of confronting one's own violence without realizing the liberating love which is bound up in this non-violent message. I may add that some non-violent movements have abandoned this source of love, this reference to liberation through love.

They make us believe that you only need to change the structures of society to eliminate all violence. Jesus begins his work of liberation by fostering revolution in the individual through his attitude of total love. Each one of us

9

should, himself, carry out this work of liberation, which, in turn, has repercussions on the structures.

The present world lives on a balance of terror, and that, perhaps, is only a colossal image of what each of us tries to live in our little personal bloc: we try to find a liveable balance between our own violence and the violence of those around us. If you come and talk of non-violence you upset this balance, everything becomes dangerous again, explosive and finally apocalyptic. Non-violence becomes a menace to everyone. It is no surprise that it is accepted neither in the East nor in the West, that it is officially allowed to reside neither with the Christians, nor with the non-Christians, nor with the atheists.

Is there not, in non-violence, an undermining force which brings down false security, which undoes the carefully hidden mechanisms of personal and collective violence, treason, and injustice, the whole series of forces that bring about panic?

**JEAN.** — 'An eye for an eye, a tooth for a tooth'. That is *lex talionis* — a way of creating a balance in vengeance. That's progress. You can't kill the other fellow just for a broken tooth. Someone breaks one of your teeth, you break one of his: are you quits? That's the illusion of violence. It's always symmetrical: you answer one murder with an other. In our civilization the 'eye for eye' has been modified, just a little. The State deals with murder. It forbids the individual to kill, keeping the right to do so for itself.

The illusion consists of believing in the balance: violence doesn't stop, it gets bigger and bigger, spirals upwards. Violence 'doesn't let itself stay still'.[7]

At the beginning of my seminars I often get the impression that I am breaking an unspoken law: if you reveal violence to people you don't do it with impunity — especially as you pass for the one who comes and accuses them of violence without getting involved. In other words, it boils down to proclaiming justice without love — doing exactly what all justices on earth do. 'If your justice is not superior to that of the scribes and the pharisees . . . what worth is it . . .' Everybody knows that justice, having either practiced it or suffered from it. 'Therefore if thou bring thy gift to the altar, and there rememberest that thy brother hath ought against thee, leave there thy gift before the altar, and go thy way; first be reconciled to thy brother, and then come and offer thy gift' (Mt 5, 23–24).

That is the justice of Jesus. When we play dirty tricks on others, the others feel them most, not we who play them. Injustices are only injustices for those who suffer from them.

Love comes before liturgy; the justice the Gospel speaks of is the indispensable basis of charity. It's not a question of being 'for' love, 'for' justice, everybody is 'for'. We bury our sins against love and justice, against other people, in silence and in compromise. Don't be surprised at what grows on that: violence, nothing else. Our sins, when they are public, should be confessed publicly. That's not masochism, it's public hygiene. If we start mutilating a little truth somewhere we always end up committing a crime later. Non-violent people have no choice but to make justice, the one the gospel talks about; they themselves can't hand it over to anyone else.

**GÉRARD.** — We really grasp only those things that concern us directly. We only feel an injustice when we undergo it. We speak only of defence at the moment it concerns us — our self-defence; we grasp much less well the defence others can put up against our own violence. We play much more willingly the role of outraged victim than of aggressor. So it is difficult for us to forgive non-violent people for upsetting our fragile structure of defence.

**JEAN.** — You just have to pronounce the word 'non-violence' to be interrupted: 'It's stupid. You've got to defend your life. So, do you let them get on with it when they come and rob you or kill you?'

For me, legitimate defence is a duty. You haven't the

11

right, in my opinion, to let yourself be killed for nothing. I'll give you the best-known example: Jesus doesn't kill the man who comes to kill him, he gives his life for him. He doesn't give it for nothing, out of cowardice, because he can see nothing else to do, because he is the weakest. No, he gives it in exchange for truth. He attacks the person in front of him with truth. The other one has a choice: he accepts that truth or he kills. There's nothing in between. There we have the aggressivity of non-violence. It really attacks man in his deepest and strongest parts: his conscience, his heart, his reason, his being.

Do you really think that on the day everyone carries a gun we'll be really safe? We confuse legitimate defence with legitimate violence. Violence, whatever it is, even if it is made legitimate by the law, can only provoke one sort of reaction: violence. In reality, legitimate violence produces a psychosis of fear, it can lead on to collective psychosis.

Under the pretext of reducing violence we feed it with our fear and our violence. How often have we read in the newspaper of a father killing his son whom he mistook for a thief, of a man shooting his neighbour whom he mistook for a prowler? I'll quote you the example of a district in Philadelphia. There were a lot of muggings, especially at night, as is the case in many big cities. The inhabitants of the district, Quakers (members of a non-violent protestant church) came up with the following solution: two people patrolled the streets from nightfall on. When they noticed any danger they gave an alarm signal; a whistle. The inhabitants of the area where the signal was heard went immediately out into the street instead of turning up the sound on the television or closing the shutters. The muggers found themselves surrounded by a crowd of people who, instead of beating them up, argued with them in a human manner: 'Why are you doing that? Are you really reduced to this sort of behaviour in order to live?' After eight months of this, people's fear was vanquished. How many muggings have taken place in subways or in trains simply because cowardice or fear had got the better of the other travellers.

I know very well that all Christian churches invoke natural law to say we have the right to defend ourselves by killing. As if the Gospel was a code of natural law!


**HILDEGARD.** — In May 1945, the Red Army invaded Vienna. My family, at the end of their tether both physically and morally, dreaded the immediate future. A dreadful reputation had gone ahead of the Russian army.

My father, Gaspard Mayr, had been one of the first non-violent people in Europe. As the Soviet troops approached our district, he unlocked our door and waited. The soldiers came in without difficulty and found themselves faced with an unarmed man. He went and got the occupants of our cellar: there were only women. They stood there, in front of the soldiers. Nothing happened. I daren't imagine what sort of result a supposedly legitimate defence would have produced. It's true that when we speak of legitimate defence we always put ourselves in a situation where the balance of power is at least equal to the aggressor's, or in our favour. That is, inwardly, we begin by changing the rules. In reality, things turn out only very rarely like that: the person who is attacked finds himself powerless, taken by surprise, just as the logic of violence intended. After all, I'm not going to attack someone I know is on the alert and stronger than me. And what about the weak, what do they do in a state of legitimate defence?


**GÉRARD.** — Now wait a minute! The pacifists, the weak precisely, are the warmongers: they make sentimental speeches about concord, and then disappear down a hole leaving the others to face the music as soon as it comes to being killed, or defending the country, or ridding the planet of madmen like Hitler. Those people refuse violence. True, their papers are full of insults for the soldiers — that doesn't take much courage. But without people

13

who are willing to get their hands dirty in order for the rest of us to live in peace, there would be no pacifists.

JEAN. — I was in the war, I was decorated because I was a good killer. I went off in 1939 because I was convinced that Hitler had to be killed. I, personally, only killed men as insignificant as myself, because the others didn't happen to be wandering around the spot where the shells were falling. Hitler also got killed, that's true — by his own hand. Forty million people had to be killed before Hitler was forced to kill himself, and so free us.

Refusing to resort to violence has nothing to do with non-violence. It's like hiding before the storm comes down on you, on the pretext that you have delicate ears. We are afraid of war because we like to keep a whole skin. When you say 'no' to violence, you say it openly, you shout it out, and accept the blows you get afterwards. Dictators don't kill people before they tell the truth, only afterwards. What was true for John the Baptist was also true for Pastor Bonhoeffer.

The pacifists you are talking about are, in fact, afraid of conflict, they dream of situations where men would no longer confront each other; they advocate tranquillity, not peace, submission, not revolution. From resignation to resignation, they end up accepting war as the least of evils; they can no longer see how it could be otherwise.

That, generally speaking, is the attitude of all the churches; they preach peace, disarmament, concord, etc., and when war breaks out they bless the guns to obtain victory. Non-violence is completely foreign to this sort of action.

GÉRARD. — If I understand correctly, you have been violent. You took part in the war. How did it go?

JEAN. — Poverty forced me to start work very young, and a young man without a real trade is easily exploited. I discovered the trade union movement out of necessity. For me, the union was the first organization I encountered which fought against injustice without arms, and which respected men.

At the age of twenty-seven I went off to war. I was decorated, I became a hero, but very soon a crushed hero. I suddenly realized that I had just buried, or even worse, betrayed, the union ideal, the ideal of respect for the human individual.

My regiment was sacrificed (we had to cover the retreat to Dunkirk). We shot, we killed as many as we could, until we were taken prisoner.

**GÉRARD.** — I am from Lorraine, I live in that part of our country which was used as a pawn during the last wars. My uncles 'defended' France in German uniform in Russia; they lost the war. Their youngest brother, my father, won the war and was part of the French occupying forces in the Rhineland. In the two wars, eighty young men from my little village were killed in Russia in German uniform. Who is going to reproach these young men for not daring to revolt against the emperor or Hitler? Not me. But what did they defend? And what did those who killed them defend?

I should add that my region is the region of the Maginot Line; it is still intact!

**JEAN.** — By our passivity, our cowardice, even by our money, we all helped those who had everything to gain from war, and who managed to get what they wanted; and we closed our ears and our eyes to reality, just as we do today with the nuclear reality.

Don't let people come and complain to us afterwards when the killings we denounce take place. We are prepared to go to prison because we say things that don't please our rulers. If we keep quiet, if we support the arms manufacturers, we won't go to prison, but our children will die at war. In Dachau museum you can see a book called *I Paid Hitler*. It was written by Fritz von Tyssen. It speaks volumes.

In the questions non-violent people are asked there are

always two aspects: on the one hand, the slap you can give or not give to the child who does something stupid, the violence of individuals we can put in the category of gangsters, and, on the other hand, war, what others do to us, given that, by definition, we always belong to a nation that does no more than defend itself. The violence which is in each one of us is evoked very rarely, and here in the West we speak very rarely of a violent economy, violent authority, violent policies, violent structures.

And yet each sort of violence corresponds to the destruction of part of the human dimension.

Violence attacks the body, mutilates, tortures, destroys man in his body. In 1981, eighty dictatorships used torture as a means of governing. The Nobel Peace prize-winner, my friend Adolfo Perez Esquivel, was tortured in Argentinian prisons in the name of 'national security', just as I was tortured by the Nazis in the name of 'security'. Violence attacks the mind, it demolishes men's souls, their ability to take up their own liberty and responsibility. Military technicians have just developed 'an ultrasonic bomb which destabilizes the human brain and can reduce the whole population of a city to idiocy'.[8] Violence attacks life by starving people to death through famine. 'Ten thousand people an hour die of hunger',[9] but they know it is because we in the West don't 'want' to save them.

Violence attacks men individually and in groups; it destroys local or national communities.

Violence is powerless before the spirit of love.

**GÉRARD.** — You aren't non-violent, since you went to war, and you killed! You were honoured by the violent ones, as they decorated you.

**JEAN.** — The butchery led me to despair, for me everything was defeat. Let me read you a letter . . .

*6th February 1980*

*My dear Edmund,*

*I would like to seize the opportunity of my stay in your little paradise to give in return, to you who have helped us so much, who have esteemed and loved us, all that is best in me, the marvel that God has put into my soul; a priceless treasure which nobody will ever be able to take away from me, but which is also hidden in every man and which every man can discover.*

*I am unable to define this Treasure, to express It. You must, in a way, surprise It in me, 'steal' It, and I never find enough 'thieves' to satisfy me. And then, this great Desire to give this Treasure grows so strong in me that I provoke them into 'stealing' It from me.*

*Out of love for you, who have given me so much, I'm going to try to put this infinite treasure into words.*

*One day, right in the depths of the world war, in 1940, not long before I was taken prisoner, I suddenly woke up feeling as if I was outside myself: an immense Force of peace and joy was flowing gently into me: I was so happy I wanted to shout with happiness, full of confidence, certainty and absolute peace; completely incomprehensible, since I was in the midst of war. It was as if I were floating above my fellow men, who all seemed to be racing after something, avidly grasping whatever they could lay hands on. At the same time, an immense love for them flowed into my soul: I loved them! And then began the enormous desire to give them this infinite happiness which penetrated me: how could I give them this happiness? How could I save them from themselves, from their greed which enslaved them and made them so miserable? Yes, how?*

*And the answer was given me, clear and precise! It was like a gentle, powerful force which opened me up beyond all my limits. Without touching, hearing or seeing a thing, this Force made me understand this: 'I am Their Father, to all these men! I am Their Creator! I have created them in an immense Love solely for them to be totally happy in all possible ways. I love them beyond everything you can imagine! I have created them for ever. I have created them for them to become God like Me, to become*

God with Me. That is, for them to love as I have loved them, even giving My Life for each one of them, so much did I love them. And I would begin again, if necessary, for I love them today as much as I did two thousand years ago, for I am The Unchangeable! ... But they don't know it. That's why they kill each other instead of loving one another. And yet only that can save them. Teach them to love each other as I love them. Teach that to them quickly! Only that can make them happy and give them the Happiness for which I created them and saved them by shedding My Blood for each one of them.'

All that was so strong, so overwhelming in me ... and I was so unable to express it that I said nothing for years, for I couldn't find words to express, to define all That. And every time, within me, I felt the urge to say It, as soon as I began to speak, everyone laughed or poked fun at me. Everyone, except, from time to time, a few who were overwhelmed by what I had to say, such as the German staff officer who saved my life twice; Cardinal Ottaviani, who refused to condemn me in spite of the scandal caused by my outspoken statements; in Russia, Commisar Jewsky, the minister for Religions, the Bishop of Moscow; in Latin America, Dom Helder Camara, Cardinal Pablo Evaristo Arns, Cardinal Aloisio Lorscheider. ...

Now what I say, or what I would like to say to people, is very simple. God, Their Creator, Their Heavenly, Eternal Father, is madly in love with them, with infinite tenderness! So much that He died on the Cross for Love of each one of them! That we are made to love Him as He himself is; He lives only to love us, to fill us 'till the cup runs over' with Happiness and Joy, that is, all of Himself, all of His Love (that same Love that you love, that you are looking for, that you would like to see, find, discover, that you felt in Cardinal Pablo Arns of Sao Paulo). God is nothing but Love! He is love! that is, Life, truth, justice! HE is EVERYTHING! And that goes for everybody.

That is the whole of my commitment, all my truth!

*I have nothing else: GOD LOVES US!.... That's the whole of my life and my continual joy! And I do my best to love, like Him, all beings, beginning with those He gave me, my own, whom I try to fulfil with all my love. But my poor little love can't fulfil them, no more than the love of all men. Their heart, their soul, their being, is much too big. We need the immense Love of God to satisfy us. That's why no creature can satisfy the human being. It can only be one of the paths that lead to God, that is, to Him who only can fulfil man. And, as soon as he finds Him he is fulfilled and so mad with Joy! And he can love all beings and give himself up entirely, for he has everything! Indeed, what more can a man ask for than to be loved totally and completely by the person he loves? Is there a greater happiness in the world? Now, if the person he adores is the most beautiful, the most intelligent, the richest, the best of all creation! If he is madly in love with him or her, to the point of dying for him or her, to the point of giving his life in the greatest of suffering!...  
Even more ... If He is God Himself, Love Himself, Wisdom and Knowledge, Truth and Life, and He is able, in His Infinite Power, to make us into BEINGS like HIM capable of loving and giving themselves entirely to everyone, to the smallest as well as the poorest!... Well yes, that happiness surpasses our understanding, and that's why men can't believe in it. They can't imagine the Reality, the Truth of what IS! They can't imagine a God so Great, so Good, so Powerful! But as soon as they discover that, that God as soon as they know that truth, they are crazy with Joy and their Happiness surpasses everything they can imagine!*

*Yes, in His never-changing wisdom, The Supreme Being, The All-Powerful, Justice, Mercy, Goodness Himself, is waiting for us at the end of this earthly life, in total respect of our liberty and of all our being, to fulfil us with His Love, with all His being! That is what God granted me, to give It to all people to whom He sends me, so that already here on earth they can make others happy and be happy like me.*

*That is all I have! But I would like to give it to you with all my heart*

*Your brother who loves you with all his heart, but didn't know how to tell you,*

*Jean Goss*

**HILDEGARD.** — I want to read to you the story of the Visitation in the Gospel of Luke (1.39–45).

'And Mary arose in those days, and went into the hill country with haste, into a city of Judea; and entered into the house of Zacharius and saluted Elizabeth. And it came to pass, that when Elizabeth heard the salutation of Mary, the babe leaped in her womb; and Elizabeth was filled with the Holy Ghost: and she spake out with a loud voice, and said, "Blessed art thou among women, and blessed is the fruit of thy womb. And whence is this to me, that the mother of my Lord should come to me? For lo, as soon as the voice of thy salutation sounded in mine ears, the babe leaped in my womb for joy. And blessed is she that believed: for there shall be a performance of those things which were told her from the Lord." '

It is as if He is saying, 'It is the very moment when you begin your life of love on earth, the moment you meet me, when you are in me. For you it is always time, but for me, poor and distracted as I am, when I realize the significance of your birth in me, there is a flash of joy, a moment of love which wipes out all my darkness and all the darkness of the world. You are there, you are everything in us, we are you. Make me poor, so that through me your kingdom of love and justice can come into being in the world, that I may become the bearer of you, of your Gospel, next to which all riches, all powers are nothing.'

During my life I have come up against all the powers of this world. I was ten when Hitler came to Vienna, my birthplace. My teacher had forced me to go with my classmates into the Ring, the main boulevard. There, in the middle of an enormous crowd, I felt the diabolical power of that man; he fascinated the crowd. Within me, a voice was shouting: 'No, I don't want to acclaim him, I don't want to welcome him, even if I am killed on the spot!' It was my first encounter with dictatorship, with the power of evil in the world. It marked me for the rest of my life. For my country, for us Austrians, the First World War was the end of an empire; the beginning of the second marked the end of a civilization. Everything collapsed. And I wonder if, even today, we are still not deeply wounded in our hearts from these successive defeats.

In Austria the suicide rate is the highest in Europe. All this has left us with a distrust of life. I had put my finger on the meaninglessness of life, like some young people today. For them, materialism opens its mocking void; for me it was the destructive, absurd violation of war, concentration camps and the dead piled up in the street. I fear this void, not death. I love death; it will give me life, true life. I have never loved life like Jean, for example. I accepted my life, accepted living it, when it became clear to me that it had a meaning because of Christ who is here in me, who is stronger than death.

Thanks to my father, I discovered that beyond the disasters and the meaninglessness, my life could serve to re-establish love in a world of hate and division.

My father, Bavarian by origin, was in opposition to Hitler. He had helped to found the International Fellowship of Reconciliation. We used to live in anguish, because we knew what was happening in Dachau and the risks our family was running. But in that torment I felt the presence of God. Even when I was a child I experienced both the meaninglessness of life and the tenderness of God. Both were in me. I lived both of them, without analysing them, of course. You had to live through faith in order to live at all.

JEAN. — Do you realize it was only three years ago, during a retreat, that I heard her say that for the first time. I couldn't believe my ears. I knew very well we didn't see eye to eye as far as life was concerned. For me, life is written with a capital L; it's God, life; and the meaning of life is: Living. What makes us live is not what happens during our life, but the original flame that burns within us.

**HILDEGARD.** — It was only when I was in my late thirties that I felt capable of giving names to all my unknown faces. That was the age at which I could look despair in the eye. The despair of seeing love betrayed by men's liberty, love destroyed by violence. I know I can only live through love, for love. If the Lord took away that faith, everything would be finished. I'd have nothing left but to kill myself. It was with Jean that I felt and discovered the force of life. From the beginning of our acquaintance I felt in him the faith of the young church after Pentecost. His faith is that of someone who has risen from death. It was entirely new for me. The Holy Spirit came into my life with Jean. He breathed confidence, joy and the strength of life into me. God takes on another face as we walk with Him. He is Jehovah, he is crucified and ends up walking with us on the night road to Emmaus.

Non-violence is nothing else than this path of love with *SOMEONE*. It's not just another philosophical or political theory. Each encounter with Him is a new departure. Each departure is a road that passes by Calvary, but leads us to Easter Sunday.

**GÉRARD.** — For both of you, non-violence is quite simply another way of saying Love — but Love as it is in the Gospel. For Hildegard, the 'revelation' has been, we could say, gentle, in contrast to Jean who has experienced the lightning stroke of Divine Love. Be it a river or a torrent, the water is the same.

But for many people, there isn't this Other One, completely Other, who overthrows you, there is only man. 'Man will have to wake up from his age-old dream and discover his total solitude, his radical strangeness. He now knows that, like a gypsy, he is marginal to the universe in which he has to live.'[10] Can non-violence have a meaning for atheists, marxists or Buddhists?

**JEAN.** — Monod, whom you have just quoted, was an atheist, but when he talks about the 'radical strangeness' of man, what does he say? 'Man is the unique value in the world, in the universe there is no other value than him.' He says it's about time we began to realize it. The scientist wanted to talk about the absurdity of human existence, I suppose, I don't know, I haven't read his book. But in my eyes he shows clearly that human existence is absurd if it is put on the same footing as other existences in the universe. There, I agree with him. Man's place is not just one among many others. God gave his life for man, not for fleas or elephants. All values arise from man, and from him only, so much for solitude. Man is an absolute. He's the only absolute, we've just found that out. But there are still people who live in another age. You see, they don't yet know that man is unique, absolute. They forget that a foetus is a man; a madman is still a man; an invalid is a man; the enemy is a man. But to realize all that, you, yourself, must give yourself. You aren't going to give yourself for the boss, the policeman or the banker, are you? Isn't the boss, the man who exploits you, a man? Isn't the Russian a man? Isn't the Black dying of hunger because he can't do anything, a man? And isn't the fellow who doesn't agree with you, who doesn't live by the same standards as you a man?

In my opinion you become a man when you stop cutting the world in two — good, bad; friends, enemies — when you finally manage to see and to respect only man.

**HILDEGARD.** — We got in touch with the countries of the Eastern bloc because, as non-violent people we couldn't accept a world cut up into sectors, into political, economical social or religious slices.

From our very first contacts with the inhabitants of the Eastern bloc countries we were confronted with this command: 'I say unto you, Love your enemies' (Mt. 5,44).

23

In 1961 we wanted to organize a meeting between Catholics and Orthodox in Yugoslavia. The war had dug a deep wound of hatred between the communities; reconciliation was impossible, humanly impossible, up till the moment when each group, in front of the others, began to admit how much they had fallen short of the Gospel.

In 1959 there was a Communist youth festival in Vienna. For Austrians, as for many Europeans or Catholics, communism is the enemy, and communists are your enemies. Someone suggested putting on a counter-festival. Instead of that, we invited the Communists to our homes; we opened our doors to them. As a result we were invited to the festival in Moscow. For the majority of Communists, a Christian is nothing better than a traitor. Religion betrays man, betrays progress. I was invited to an evening on Youth and Religion at the Writers' Club. The room was packed and hostile. The organizers had just been projecting ridiculously stupid films discrediting religion, and then, magnanimously, gave five minutes to the 'officiants' of the religions officially recognized in the USSR to talk about 'their' religion.

I was there, knowing I had to speak, but feeling that the task was beyond me. I spoke: 'If I am here it is because I believe in you. You are Communists because you want with all your strength to promote justice for men of our time; you have committed your life to that philosophy, and you are not here just for fun. My friends and I are Christians. We are not here to play. In the name of the Gospel, we are trying to be true to man. We are struggling to stop the Algerian war, we are struggling to resolve conflicts other than by murder.

'That force which moves us, which moves you, too, is the same, it makes us into men worthy of the name.'

I added that we had very often not been true to the Gospel, and I asked them if they didn't have any questions to put to themselves about their own fidelity. The five minutes ran into twenty.

Years later we met some young people from that evening. The seed had grown wonderfully. We also know that it produced some martyrs.

In each one of us there is violence; but in each one of us, whatever our faith, we have the capacity to act through love, with justice and for truth. 'The dividing line between good and evil passes through the heart of every man. And who is willing to destroy part of his own heart?'[11]

# II

**GÉRARD.** — You have just borne witness to the fact that non-violence concerns people who have a certain religious or human faith, that is, people who have faith in man. Your own experience shows that not only does non-violence not harm man, but demands the love of man, including our enemies. The enemy is not just the adversary. He's not just fighting against you, he has only one goal: to do you harm, and, if necessary, kill you. It is possible to respect your adversary; at a pinch, to love him, but do you think it is reasonable to ask people to love someone who wants to destroy them, especially since, generally speaking, enemies respect neither faith nor law, and act out of thirst for power and wealth, with no other ideology than their pocket's?

**JEAN.** — Not only does non-violence demand that we love our enemies, but it is also based on the love of enemies. It goes even further. The non-violent person gives his life for his enemies. I fully agree with you, it's not reasonable. As if Love could be measured by what is reasonable or not. As soon as you love, no matter who, you do three things: you don't accept violence, you accept the loved one with absolute generosity, and you accept the suffering he imposes on you, because you love him; so you attack his conscience until he comes aware of the evil he is doing you.

On the 1st December 1955, a black dressmaker, Mrs Rose Parks, was sitting with sore feet in a place reserved for Whites on a Montgomery City Bus Line bus. A white man got in and demanded his seat. Mrs

Parks' refusal meant she was charged on the spot. That was the beginning of the bus boycott by the black population of Montgomery.

A grandmother was limping along, and some Whites laughed at her, saying: 'Well old lady, aren't you tired of walking?' 'Oh yes' she answered, 'my old legs can hardly go any further, but I'm walking for my grandchildren, so that they can be free one day. And then I'm walking out of repentance for my sin, my cowardice at having taken part for so long in the injustice of segregation, at having tolerated it. I'm also walking for you. When I've paid for you, just as Jesus paid for us all on the Cross, you Whites will also understand the injustice that we Blacks understand so well.[12]

The bus company had only one ethic: profit. The Blacks' victory, however, went further than buses. On the 20th December, 1956, a ruling from the United States Supreme Court proved the Blacks right; segregation in buses was anticonstitutional.

Martin Luther King appealed to the Blacks at that moment: 'May our return to the buses be accompanied with enough love to transform an enemy into a friend.'[13]

But an ideology can't bring that about. Ideologies are inhuman monsters, even if they have humanitarian names. All ideologies end up killing people. If you separate love from non-violence you turn non-violence into an ideology, a gimmick. Structures that are not inhabited by justice and love have no liberating or reconciling force, and are never sources of life.

For me, love for our enemies is the creative, liberating love of God incarnated in ourselves; it frees the oppressed and the oppressor at the same time. Of course, if you go round talking like that people take you for someone who has left this planet for good. I always hear myself saying: 'You're not with it, Jean. We know very well, it's written in the Gospel, but it's impossible, idealistic, a utopia. So

27

come along, put on your lead-soled shoes and come back to good old gravity.'

Right. So I come back and I open my eyes. The Americans, the British, the Russians and the French freed the world of Hitler and the Nazi plague. And then . . . the Russians carried on with their gulag, the Americans went to war in Vietnam and My Lai, the British still torture the Irish even today, and France fought and tortured in Algeria. That's reality. Just a bit of it, because all these rich countries have turned the world into a concentration camp in which fear reigns for some, famine and poverty for others.

We don't notice it so much here in the West, because we are among those who benefit by it. What I mean is that by using nazism's own methods to get rid of nazism, we have been poisoned by it; nazism has been replaced by more modern forms of violence. The result is always the same.

If we refuse to heap burning coals onto our enemies, that is, to set fire to their consciences with our own capacity for loving, they will never realize what they are doing. What's more, our abdication will ruin everything creative and free in love. Even if you cut them off, the heads of violence will grow again and again.

**HILDEGARD.** — The American troops came into the village in Bavaria where my father was born, and imprisoned a young man I knew well because they suspected him of possessing weapons. As I could speak a little English I had to act as interpreter between the young man and the occupying forces. The Americans wanted to shoot him. I was shaking with fear, and also with disgust. I remember my disappointment very well: 'So they do the same as Hitler's people!' A soldier came the following day and offered me a big bottle of wine to 'wipe my fear away', as he said. The young man had escaped death. Violence knows no face, it has only victims. Love sees faces which cry out and which are never the same.

Do you think that a mother exists who would react

differently to the one in the judgement of Solomon? We have two children, Etienne and Myriam. If, by misfortune, they were to fight, can you imagine even for a moment that Jean and I would look on as mere spectators, or help one to kill the other? It's unthinkable; we would intervene; we would do anything to stop the war; we would put ourselves in between them; we would risk our lives for them, and that would be perfectly normal and natural. The two women who argue over a child in front of the king are prostitutes. The false mother is willing to have the child killed rather than lose it. What she wanted was not the child, but possession. The true mother, the one who gave it life, rejects the murder; she wants her child to live. Love of the enemy exists in the Old Testament. It has been in existence for a long time, but there's one thing we must say clearly — we are talking about love, not some little self-willed virtue growing in our minds, watered with moralizing theories. They were prostitutes. . . .

We have removed love for enemies from the Gospel, to replace it with realism. All right! The Gospel is an abandoned shack, and all we need do is put up a notice saying: 'For sale, empty house'.

'Love of enemies' could also mean 'freeing men from their violence.' Relations between men cannot be established on spilt blood. God 'can only make himself known to men if he gets from them what Jesus offers them, that which makes up, without reservations or sacrificial intermediary, the essential theme of his teaching; a reconciliation which allows God to reveal himself as he is for the first time in the history of mankind.[14] In fact Jesus says: 'Love your enemies . . . that ye may be the children of your Father which is in heaven: for he maketh the sun to rise on the evil and on the good . . .' (Matt 5. 44–45).

GÉRARD. — We are faced yet again with this pillage of the Gospel by those very people we are supposed to be its guardians: us christians. To look at us, I wonder if we aren't afraid we might find something inadmissible in the Gospel which would force us to give up completely: aren't we afraid to find a face of God beneath the Beatitudes impossible to look upon? In the Old Testament, God is far from always being a father, and deep down inside us the Sacrifice of Christ to reconcile us with the Father looks very much like a bloodthirsty deed. We try hard to excuse the God of the Old Testament. When he talks well, we say 'That's God'. When things don't fit in with our notion of God as Love, we find all sorts of excuses for him, but we stay within the Old Testament.

We don't touch the New Testament; we creep around it, getting love of enemies out of the way in one corner, nibbling at absolute respect for human life in another, slipping legitimate defence into the breach we have just made — all that so as not to touch the centre: the sacrifice of Christ demanded by his Father.

I mean to say, what did Christ free us from? From violence? . . . But just have a look round you: 'He sacrificed himself for me'. Ah, no, stop that! I never asked for anything. Me, responsible for his death? But that's going too far, who gave you the right to accuse me? All that remains hidden in our hearts, and we cover it up with bits of moral debris we have picked up here and there in order to keep a utilitarian façade for the Gospel, and especially for the Christian edifice behind it

How do you expect Christians to be non-violent when they are convinced that their God is violent, because he demands the blood of Isaac and the blood of Jesus in order to finally feel kindly disposed towards us?

**JEAN.** — Now we're getting down to it. When I came back from captivity I 'knew' Jesus Christ. I saw only him, I knew nothing else. Now just imagine what happened in my mind when I heard about the Father, when I began to realize how much went on in people's hearts concerning God's violence, his love of vengeance and his taste for blood. I went to see the director of *Etudes*, Father Ridot, I contacted Pastor Lasserre, of the French Reformed Church, and others, in order to study this question. It's not that I wanted to set up a new bible school, but I realized that Christians had a problem in that respect. I couldn't see God as infinite power, an infinite, transcendent being. I had known Jesus; there was no going back.

'He who has seen me has seen the Father.' I saw love, I lived on it every day, every minute of my life, so it was unthinkable that there should be 'anything else' in God but love. Because I now understand what happens in the hearts of some people when they read the Bible. God has two faces. On the one hand, he is kind; on the other, he is the savage who orders the extermination of children and promises himself the massacres of the Apocalypse.

Now we are made in that image; we only need to look ourselves in the eye for a couple of minutes. I understand why Jesus passes for a dreamer, a utopian, and all non-violent people with him. 'Do what you want, there will always be wars,' say the learned Christians along with others who are not Christian. I translate that like this: God will always be bastard enough to let us die shamefully because he doesn't like the look of us or because he has a bad temper. Frankly, if you had it in your power, and if you weren't completely perverted, would you let war break out? Would you put up with that? Certainly not! Then is God worse than you? And then there are the others: God is good. All goodness comes from God. You can see what is left for man: Evil. But where is the God who was overcome by Jacob and was made man? Through death on the Cross, God suffered violence. We just have to do the same. And God the Father organizes the macabre spectacle of his son being put to death. It makes you want to scream. Jean-Michel Oughourlian says in Girard's book: 'To justify the sacrificial reading, of which there is no mention in the Gospels, we are obliged to postulate a sort of agreement between the father and the son which remains secret and which concerns the sacrifice in question. The Father, for reasons which remain obscure to us, asks the Son to sacrifice himself, and the Son, for reasons equally obscure, obeys this injunction worthy of Aztec gods. In short, we are talking of a secret agreement on matters concerning violence, of the sort that could exist nowadays between superpowers sometimes obliged to come to an understanding without consulting their people.'[15]

Christ provokes his arrest and his death sentence by his attitude. Go and tell the truth in public places and you will soon see what happens to you! For thirty years Jesus says nothing; he attacks nobody's conscience. But the moment comes; God reveals himself. Jesus attacks the consciences of the Jews, the Romans, the Samaritans and the pagans. He rejects any pact with lies or lying structures. He regularly provokes those in power, those who produce injustice and those who crush their fellow men, for whatever pretext. He brings division. 'I am not come to bring peace but the sword.' He tells the Father's truth to all men, and he backs up this truth with all his life and his blood.

What man doesn't think in terms of violence to justify himself, and includes God in his justification? *Gott mit uns* (God with us) is an old idea, and it is not just written on German army belt buckles . . .

He causes a scandal when he states God's truth: Love. Love transcends murder: 'You can kill me, I love you.' 'Hereby perceive we the love of God, because he laid down his life for us. And we ought to lay down our lives for the brethren' (1 John 3.16).

HILDEGARD. — The poor the world over were taught resignation and acceptance of suffering as a down-payment on rewards to be received in the other world. The suffering we are talking about, the one Christ had to undergo, was the consequence of what he bore witness to 'because continuing to live would signify submission to violence.'[16] I felt that very strongly in South America. The suffering which is the consequence of our commitment, the price we have to pay, is shouldered willingly so as to bring about a fraternal life, a life worthy of man. The kingdom will not come within me just because I have passively accepted the conditions of sin. It will come only in so far as I have been faithful to the evangelical injunc-

tion to transfigure the world. Because of the witness I
have borne, a cross will inexorably come down onto my
shoulders, but it will also weigh with all its weight on the
shoulders of my adversaries, because it will bear a weight
of love and not a weight of hatred. 'Blessed are you that
are persecuted in my name.' If it is not in his name it is
false, I fall into the trap of lies or pagan sacrifice. In our
life that is the question we put to ourselves every day: 'Is
it because of him?' If it is not because of him we regress
into paganism. And what Jesus says is *true*: there can be
Joy in the midst of persecution.

**GÉRARD.** — Dear unbelieving reader, you may well
feel that the paragraph you have just read doesn't concern
you. 'After all, the Gospel is Christians' business; they'll
just have to sort out their problems among themselves:
they are nothing to do with me.' That shows you don't
know non-violent people very well. The god we are talking
about, the one with two faces, one which smiles and one
which terrifies, the god who swallows up his victims, who
'allows' massacres to take place, is also yours. You say
you don't know this god? Of course you do, I'll tell you
his name: *power*. When you are well in with him, he
smiles at you; when he has gone off you, you die; of
hunger, thirst or torture. How many fathers have sacrificed
their sons to this god; not only their sons but all the rest
of the family. Thank you for having paused a minute with
me. If you wish we will carry on.
Listening to you I am surprised at the way you speak
of the Gospel as truth, as *the truth*. I, Jean Goss, I tell you
the truth. There is no other, and I find this truth in the
Gospel, and it applies to everybody. That's enough to
make anyone panic. Truth has become tainted merchan-
dise; everyone is selling it; all ideologies, all philosophies
and all religions have it out on show.

**JEAN.** — That's true, but mine can't be found in any
shop window because you only find dummies in shop
windows; the truth we are talking about is Someone. With

our truth, you can't just take it and sit on it. Truth is very simple; man is the supreme value and from him spring all other values. The truth I'm talking about is you, it's Hildegard, it's me; it isn't some all-knowing star out there at the back end of the universe. Pilate asks the question: 'What is truth?' We can understand Jesus' silence. Truth isn't a thing; truth is *him*. I often get the impression that we imagine truth to be a pile of stones we stumble up to, blind as we are, in the hope of filling our pockets with them. Those truths are made to be thrown at the first heretic to come along. You know, everybody is always somebody else's heretic. When truth is a thing you can possess it, and he who says 'have' says 'defend'. You just have to follow the argument; we defend by killing. We kill provided the truth remains in our possession. The truth we have in our hearts has no need to be defended, it needs witnesses, and the Greek for witness is 'martyr'.

Gandhi said: 'Truth contains love, and firmness springs from it: and so its synonym is strength.' Non-violence is strength born of love and truth. This strength is 'an attribute of the spirit which is in each one of us.'[17]

And finally, for me, truth is Christ, and He comes to us more quickly than we go to him. The whole world could say to me 'You're wrong, that's not truth; as for men, you can kill them, it's as if you were pouring water on a rock. It just doesn't soak in.' I know, but not through my intellect. I know with all my being that God is, that he loves man, and that the man in question is sacred, that, under no circumstances, have we the right to lie to him, exploit him or torture him; that under no circumstances can we kill him. I'm sure that's God's truth.

The Gospel says it on every page. That's the truth I'm going to repeat to all men, to all the Vaticans in the world. Oh, they're not really against it, generally speaking, but they think it's a bit ahead of its time. You see what I mean, it's Vatican III.

GÉRARD. — When you speak of the roots of non-violence — love, truth and justice — you always refer to your own personal experience, which is itself profoundly tied up in your relationship with the God of the Gospel. We tend to live in a completely different way. To find out what we must think or do, we look for the answer on the shelves of different religious or philosophical theories. You want to know what I think? Go and ask Rome or Moscow, or the latest 'guru'. It would be wonderfully practical if non-violence had a code, or an instructions handbook, but I haven't much hope in that respect. Fortunately, perhaps.

**HILDEGARD.** — That's true, non-violence is based on the awareness of our ability to act out of love for justice, and in truth.

Love is a fundamental human experience through which you live both in your own eyes and in the eyes of others, and this existence is total. You aren't a plumber or a teacher; no, in love you is you. The loved one is always the only one. Love is the most tremendous, creative force in the world, and to create it draws on its own energy, which never runs dry. Non-violence is creative at all levels. It 'creates' man by rejecting all mutilations and alienations, be they political, economic or religious. Non-violence is creative on the social level because it introduces truth into human relations instead of chains forged by force. On the economic level it creates justice because its reference is total man.

I would like to give two examples of non-violent struggles which are taking place at this moment (1981).

In 1976, Mairead Corrigan and Betty Williams, two Irishwomen, created the Peace People movement. Mairead's sister and three of her children were killed by a truck during a confrontation between Catholics and the peace-keeping forces. Catholic and Protestant Irishwomen went out into the streets to say 'no' to violence. There was the Nobel Prize, and then the movement started to go to pieces. Betty Williams even left the movement, but her companion continued. The magic of the demonstration faded away, they had to get down to the everyday business of fighting for peace; fighting against violent laws and torture in prison. Justice was still only a distant hope. For Mairead Corrigan 'we must get rid of this fear that paralyses everything.'[18] In her eyes 'the I.R.A. is only interested in violence. In 1976 civil war was only just avoided. The Irish people are not terrorists; terrorists are five per cent of the population.' And, 'We must arrange things so that the majority of the population has the right to speak,' says Mairead, 'and not just a violent minority, which will once more impose its will through violence. Our duty is to bring people together in order to find suitable political structures, to find solutions to the question of independence and unity at the same time. We must first of all create an atmosphere of dialogue. Some people find it slow, that's true, we are working from day to day.' In Mairead's eyes this painstaking work is more important than what she was doing in 1976. A people tries to break through the wall of contradictions, fear and injustice which surrounds them; women, having no doubt avoided the worst, patiently set about creating a new society because non-violent combat goes well beyond the departure of the English. When they go, they will still leave the Protestants behind on the island, and they too have the right to live! Non-violent struggle goes well beyond the short-term goals violent struggles generally set themselves. Get rid of the king, and everything will be all right; kill Stalin and all the problems will be solved. In non-violent struggle man appears for what he is, growing slowly and painfully, but he appears none the less; he is born. In violence, he dies.

Lech Walesa . . . everyone knows of him, but how many people know that he has been struggling for twelve years, and has had to put up with all sorts of situations, all sorts of prisons? He says: 'You can degrade a man in several ways. I have known a few. Each time, it was men who degraded me. Men more than the system.' For him the effectiveness of Solidarity can be explained in just one way: 'Because I tell the truth, whatever the system. If you don't base your action on truth and honesty, you haven't got a chance. Truth is man; you can do nothing against truth; you can't destroy it.'[19] Imagine a second Walesa with a weapon in his hands, what would he have achieved? What would he have created? Greater liberty and well-being for the Polish workers? I know his determination and his faith, his absence of fear, too, even in the face of Soviet tanks. I also know the source of all his energy: Jesus Christ.

'Against the well-planned world strategy of communism only spiritual factors can come to the aid of the West; there are no others,' said Solzhenitsyn to the Harvard students in 1978.[20] That's true for communism, and for capitalism, too, and remains true for the fight against all evil that comes from man, against all forms of violence. But there you are; here, in the West, we only believe in bombs. It is marvellous to see that the Polish Church, Czechoslovak Catholics and Protestants are openly engaged in non-violent struggles, the only ones which respect all men, including the oppressors.

**GÉRARD.** — Listening to you and, even more, knowing and loving you, it's clear that your non-violence finds its source in an experience built up over the years. With Hildegard it runs deeply and comes calmly to the surface; with you, Jean, it surges up and boils over. Nothing has aged over the years; non-violence has penetrated all the corners of your hearts and your lives. It pierces through the whole person, to that inner core which makes us really live.

It's a total experience of life.

**JEAN.** — Non-violence, like the Gospel, is not an ideal, a sort of sausage continually dangling just in front of my nose, and moving just out of reach every time I take a step towards it. By 'idealizing' the Gospel we make it absolutely unliveable, and we expel it into interstellar space, where there are no more men, and no more conflicts, where only frigid ideas reign.

**GÉRARD.** — I know you have been along that road, and I admire you for being so free and so little disappointed.

**HILDEGARD.** — I can't manage to live non-violence, but I am happy to know that the Lord uses me as best he can, with all my weaknesses and all my cowardices.

**JEAN.** — I have been trying to live non-violence for forty years, and I haven't managed it. I have hit my children, so you can see what a failure it was for me! Disappointed? Yes, by myself, that's all. But just because Peter denies his master three times, does that mean his master doesn't love him?

**HILDEGARD.** — My patron saint, Hildegard of Bingen (12th century), has marked me deeply. She preached in the churches and helped women to give birth. There were heretics at that time who were condemned by the church. But she, the abbess of a convent, buried a heretic in the cemetery because she thought that this man, who had followed his conscience, should be judged by God, and not by men.

The bishop withdrew the holy sacrament from her, but she held on. It's true that the path of non-violence in us is a path that leads to the depths, and a way of liberation. How can you help others to be free if you yourself are tied up in your good-bad, friend-enemy syndrome? Impossible! Jesus' liberating message has been stifled, reduced to pious mouthings reserved for people who live in ivory towers into which evil never penetrates, and where conflicts are no more than theological 'disputes'. I am cowardly, I am unfaithful to non-violence and love. But *He* is faithful, absolutely faithful. My shadowy areas are there. They do not allow me to condemn my enemy's darkness. When I manage to accept them, I have not performed an act of willed heroism, I have let myself be loved, and at that moment I can also love, and at that moment I can also love the person I have in front of me. He is also a bearer of God's breath. My enemy is like me, alienated, enslaved by evil and, like me, he needs liberation. Liberation comes about in the same breath for my enemy and for me. That's what non-violent morality is about.

# III

**JEAN.** — Morality is a question of love. Who does morality concern? Man. And man is sacred because he is loved by God. Good is not abstract because as soon as good becomes something abstract, you give yourself the right to kill in order to keep it. Men have been killed, and continue to be killed, in the name of God because God, too, has become an abstraction. God has become an idol, and idols demand bloody sacrifices, preferably human! Idols are not just ancient history; their names are power, money, multinationals. The god who has become just a word has no meaning for me any more; and when good, too, has become just a word, then man is destroyed.

**HILDEGARD.** — When good becomes a thing, the dictatorship of virtue is not far off. Since it is good, it must be imposed. As the Gospel is the best there is, let's impose it. We'll end up imposing non-violence . . . by violence. Neither the law nor the letter gives the spirit, it's the other way round; the spirit gives meaning to the law and the letter. And the Spirit is the Spirit of Love.

**GÉRARD.** — Moral structures remind me of the hero of Kafka's *Metamorphosis:* a man wakes up one morning imprisoned in a beetle's hard shell, which cuts him off completely from other people, making all communication impossible — like the pharisees' shell that Jesus attacks. We all build walls around ourselves and mount guard behind our morality, ready to fire at the first attacker to come along. When the attacker is the prophet, he who speaks in the name of the Lord, then we shoot him down.

**JEAN.** — Morality without love is a machine for imposing on people, for dominating them. We need a word, a living communication; codes are made for judges, not for living people. It is the intellectuals who bring about this perversion of the Word into a code, and who then impose it. And what's more, they make you feel guilty: 'Ah! you're not following *the* line. You are in a state of sin!' And there you are, the circle is closed; you can't do anything about it. The word is not imposed from the outside, it is sown in us, and either it germinates and flourishes or it doesn't, that's not my business; but it can't be transformed into love if it doesn't become our word and our law.

Non-violence becomes non-violence only if it has germinated in our hearts and risen from our depths. It's not a collection of recipes made for 'good little boys': it's the flowering of all our being — in spite of our handicaps. What I'm saying is not particularly new. In a loving family, are the faults of one or the other of the members reserved for use in quarrels, or does love include these faults? What is true for love is always true universally. The non-violent person accepts conflict. He confronts it in himself and round about him.

Jesus' attitudes are characteristic. He sees Zacheus and invites himself to his home; the pharisees wouldn't have dared do that. Really, a swine like him! Go and eat as a friend in his house? He would do better to change his life, and then after that we'll see! Disclose the secret of his life to a rather disreputable woman and a heretic into the bargain. Ah, no! And yet the Samaritan woman was happy, at last, to have someone tell her 'who she was'. But that still exists today. Even Christian peace movements in France don't believe that we, the supposedly Christian nations, can take the first step towards disarmament as long as the Soviet Union continues to be armed as it is. That means in so many words: 'Dear Soviet Communist Party Central Committee, apply the Gospel, and if it works we will do the same as you.'

In another field you have abortion. It's bad, it's murder,

we must forbid it. We must impose good on everyone; that's logical, isn't it? It's strange to note that, in France at least, those who want to forbid abortion are in favour of the death penalty and, inversely, those against the death penalty are for abortion. Everyone respects man! In both cases we end up with corpses . . . of men. Everything can become an idol, not just God; man and morality as well. Non-violence only accepts as God the one who beseeches our love to take him in, to become his own. Jesus dared love all those whom the moralists threw on the scrap-heap.

**GÉRARD.** — In Genesis, God gave man this order: 'Of every tree of the garden thou mayest freely eat, but of the tree of the knowledge of good and evil, thou shalt not eat of it: for in the day that thou eatest thereof thou shalt surely die' (Genesis 2, 16–17).

So you see, we have all eaten of this fruit, and we continue to eat it, instead of loving, instead of seeking life and its oneness.

**HILDEGARD.** — Jesus breaks that way of thinking which is rooted in every man and re-establishes universally equal value for all men. Jesus' liberating mission is not the struggle of the oppressed against their oppressors in order to defeat, dominate and finally wipe them out. The liberation of the oppressed affects the oppressors and carries them along in the same movement. To want to liberate and to destroy at the same time is to betray man.

**JEAN.** — 'No one in the world can sink so low that he cannot be converted by love.'[21] But the illusion is to think that the conversion takes place through my action. Just because I have attacked my adversary with all the love I am capable of, that doesn't mean he's going to fling his arms round my neck and say: 'Jean, you're right'. That would be a success, but less than a conversion. It has happened, it's true, I've seen it: after a lot of suffering a rich Brazilian landowner ended up accepting the division of his land.

Generally speaking, the purse puts a 'screen' between hearts, but non-violence gives the other person a chance, and no small one; the chance that he too may one day find love. It is always pleasant — and flattering — to see one's work crowned with success, but on the human scale, what does that add up to? You just have to be a mother or a father to know all about 'success'. If we use God or love as an instrument to succeed with, we'll be in for a big disappointment. The levels on which non-violence succeeds are not the same as those on which moral recipes succeed. Cesar Chavez, a Mexican, attacked the powerful Californian landowners who were maltreating their foreign workers. He fought against the trusts for years; he didn't convert the rich landowners, who gave in because of the drop in their bank balances, but he won thousands of Americans over to non-violence. The middle-class American housewives, who boycotted Delano grapes, made Chavez win. 'Every time the people of God become effective according to worldly criteria, that means society has absorbed our action and used it for itself and its own benefit.'[22]

**HILDEGARD.** — The split we maintain between good and evil, friend and enemy is extended into the way we understand Christianity here in the West. For some, Christianity is a personal, strictly ecclesiastical affair; for others it is a means to success.

I know it isn't easy to live with a Gospel that is not a book of recipes, and which takes you where you don't want to go. We are so comfortably established in our divisions; we've drawn a line and it is easy to see which side Good is on — 'our Good' — and which side those who don't think like us, or act like us are on. Jesus doesn't say 'be "united" as my Father and I are united', he says 'Be one.' That's not the end of our contradictions; they are transcended, because they take on a new sense which has nothing to do with our divisions. They become part of the oneness. Philosophy, politics or theology can not give us this oneness, can not resolve our divisions through reasoning. We need the experience of our depths. 'There is not "Him" there and "you" here; there is a unique us.'[23]

**GÉRARD.** — I think experience often takes a very simple form for those who try to live non-violence. You don't hang up non-violence when your day's work is done. Everything we live transforms us totally, and uncovers an absolutely inexhaustible supply of energy within us. Theories produce no energy, because they stay on the mental level. We don't give our lives for theories. What you call 'conscientisation', 'the call to the other's humanity', is nothing other than a call to his personal experience: you urge him to 'be'. You must admit that Jean has a rough way of urging, and I'm speaking from experience. He turned everything upside down in me . . . with a great deal of love. The little system of my life fell to pieces, and I was so much the happier. Truth has a face, you say, non-violence can't be learnt from books, it is transmitted through a face. As soon as it passes from one person to another, it becomes alive; it starts to live immediately. In a word, it is incarnated and it transforms. Coming out of a 'talk' by Jean (there is not yet an adequate word for Jean's 'verbal tempests'), the blue of the sky hadn't changed, but everything else had. I found myself encumbered with my own liberty which had become too vast for me, and struggling with fear. I no longer needed to hide my fear from myself, and suddenly I gave up all the fine words I would normally have used to wrap it up. I found myself in good company; that is, the apostles, Christ's disciples. In the Gospel, fear and faith are always directly linked. When his friends confess they are afraid, Jesus never calls them cowards, or says they lack courage. He reproaches them for their lack of faith. In our minds, fear is linked with violence, and we think we can solve the problem by a willed act: courage. Have you ever been afraid, Jean?

**JEAN.** — I am soft, I'm afraid of suffering, and can't stand heroism. That's me, that's how I am; and yet I've been tortured, I've spent days in prison, I've been humiliated. It surprises me myself, when I tell you about it, sitting comfortably in this chair. How could I have lived through all that? I can assure you that since my meeting with Christ, I have never been afraid. I've been worried, but I've never really been afraid any more. I know I could face up to the whole world. I am absolutely certain that He loves us more than we can dream, think, know or believe, that He loves us beyond all our faults. That's my faith. That sort of faith wipes away fear. And then, one day we will have to realize that it is above all He, God, who has faith in us, men. When Jesus says 'men of little faith', he reproaches us for our lack of love: 'men of little love'. If we had love as big as a mustard-seed, we would transform the world.

**GÉRARD.** — Please Jean, not so fast, and not so far. If I understand the path of non-violence correctly, we must begin by admitting our fear, admitting it to ourselves, and living with it without being ashamed: 'Almost everything in fear is fear of fear or shame of fear.'[24] However much I pull counter-arguments out of my computer-brain to hide or mask my fear, it makes no difference, it still taunts me. Fear surrounds us, reduces us to despair. Truly violent people and truly non-violent people have this in common at least: they fear nothing and nobody. And the rest of us just zigzag in between.

**HILDEGARD.** — Fear is a signal: when it shows itself it lets you know clearly you are at the door of your own prison. We fear for our existence. It's not always a matter of physical existence, it can just as well concern our existence in relation to others, that is, our economic or social existence. Think of all the sacrifices we offer the 'gods' who guarantee 'our life'.

In that case, what resonance does Jesus' word take on

– 'he who would save his life will lose it, he who would lose his life will save it'?

To admit our fear is to come up against our own wall, which shuts us up inside our little selves. He is the one that panics. The little self is our social identity label; we write on it everything we would like to be in our own eyes and in the eyes of others; we parade it up and down in the street in order to exist. If anyone touches it we die of shame. We think this label is our life; those who have accepted the destruction of this self discover with wonder that they have discovered life, and with it, liberty. Whether it is in India, Japan or here in the West, the language is the same because the experience is the same. Fear has this great advantage, that it shows us clearly where our real life is, which nothing can destroy; it puts us in contact with, makes us feel physically where the source of our existence is.

The path that leads to this source is not always very spectacular, but it always seems beyond our strength. Thomas Merton describes the 'path of the purification of the heart as a path of temptation and struggle. It demands that we overcome obstacles that seem to surpass human strength. Obstacles which do indeed surpass it'.[25] But for me, as for many people, it is Jesus' affirmation, 'I am the way, the truth and the light', which verifies our courage.

**JEAN.** — Faith, as I have explained, sweeps away fear, but it also gives one faith in oneself. The whole world, including the pope and all the bishops, can call me utopian, that won't make me change a word of what I say. Similarly, if I happen to be cowardly, it doesn't upset me. I know that the Lord will use it even if I don't know why.

People have tried very many times to tell me that man can be killed under certain conditions: scholars and theologians maintained it was just. I couldn't prove the contrary to them, but I was sure I was right, that under no circumstances had we the right to kill. I haven't changed for forty years, and I can assure you that has got me, and Hildegard, too, into trouble.

**GÉRARD.** — A few days before he died, Father Guy Riobé wrote this in *Le Monde*: 'At certain moments in its history the Church has taken fright at the Spirit, stopped being mystical and creative and become legalistic and moralizing. At these times, the squalls of the Spirit have blown round about the church, and sometimes against it, vigorously demanding creativity, justice and beauty.' That is the testament of a non-violent man. He's quite clear about it; fear reveals itself the moment the current linking us to the Spirit, to our depths, dries up. As soon as we cut off communication with our deep source, life stops, everything hardens into laws and we lose our creativity.

We are all subject to fear of the Spirit: it's the fear of being stripped and finding ourselves naked. It is hard to let go of what we have acquired with so much difficulty, and set off heaven knows where. But can we expect everyone who wants to undertake a non-violent action to make this descent into the depths of their being?

**JEAN.** — What do violent men demand? You must give your life, but you are of no importance. You're just a 'uniform'; all 'uniforms' add up to the same, men don't count, only figures. Caiaphas reasons like all military leaders, and like us all when we are violent: 'It is better that one man should die', etc. It's a question of number. We all know levelling down is necessary if you want to impose violence: 'We must bring the ringleaders to heel.' Fear is pushed to its uttermost when it makes men lose their humanity and kill each other for no reason: that's war. The creative power of non-violence 'personalizes' men and makes them live on all levels. Of course that doesn't come about by magic, it happens in a human manner, and so it is slow and unforeseen. The non-violent person is a 'humble researcher experimenting with certain eternal truths'.[26]

**HILDEGARD.** — The great eastern and western teachings are guides for man's inner liberty. They free us from the slavery to our tyrannical and fearful 'Me'; the hard, selfish shell is gradually dissolved by the warmth that comes from our heart.

Whenever men or women take this path to inner freedom, into their depths, the problem of action no longer arises for them; the problem of success or failure no longer has any meaning.

Only 'spectators' have problems of this sort: 'Is it better to throw myself into action or to contemplate my naval? Is it better to go into politics or to shut myself up in a monastery?' If we ask questions like that, then we are obviously still looking for ourselves; those who have found themselves no longer have problems like that. They just live. Too bad for those who have eyes and can't see! But one part of your question has not been answered. Violent people are freed from fear too; many people secretly admire them, and are so fascinated that many are prepared to die for them. Certain men have managed to open up sources of energy deep within themselves which give them extraordinary domination over those who surround them. These men exert a tyrannical force on people who have no personal depth. Someone who commits himself to non-violence is obliged to plumb his own depths, with all the dizzying drops and suffering this inevitably entails, and as a result is protected from the power of dictators, fine talkers and traders in political illusions.

As long as our non-violence doesn't arise from these depths we will be tossed about by such mirages, will fall into the trap of apparent success and failure and will be unable to stand up against the will of the 'powerful'.

Renouncing the 'spiritual self' leads inevitably to two catastrophes: fanaticism and destruction; and it explains very clearly what happens with the fanatic. He is possessed by anxiety, the anxiety he claims to have overcome. What does he do? He attacks with incredible violence those who do not share his dogmas, because those very unbelievers show him what he refuses to see, what he cannot bear to see: his own anguished weakness. According to one of his biographers, Hitler was an extremely anxious man. These very weaknesses, these fears that the fanatic should get rid of in his own self, but which he is incapable of doing, he feels it is his mission to get rid of in others. 'His anxiety forces him to persecute dissenters. The weakness of the fanatic is that those whom he fights have a secret hold on him; and to this weakness he and his group finally succumb'.[27] Graf Durkheim explains: 'The more the self puffs up with pride, drawing on the forces of the *hara* (man's vital centre), the more the magician loses true power born of contact with the being'.[28]

When the strength and the moderation that came from this contact are lacking, he has to substitute the original burst of energy with a deliberate will for power which leads him inevitably to his 'own destruction'.

Our fascination with violent people stops as soon as we take the path into our own being, into what we really are; it stops as soon as we take the path of non-violence.

**GÉRARD.** — This path into ourselves is often indicated by an other which grows within us and which loves us. We can all experience that, and its opposite; hatred. The other person's malice can make us feel 'beside ourselves' with anger. The expression is true in all senses of the word. Love presents the other one with a reflection of his own true nature, his depths; and that goes for love of one's enemy, too. But there are so many falls on the way, so many knocks. We think we have hold of something to help us up, only to see it collapse. In order to enter non-violence must we give up everything and make a vow of poverty?

**JEAN.** — When I met Hildegard I was committed to non-violence up to the hilt, and so was she. In fact I had two commitments: one to non-violence, for which I was prepared to lay down my life, and one to poverty. I wanted to live like Jesus: love men totally with the strength that comes from poverty. He never killed and never took anything from anyone; he lived with the strict minimum. I couldn't imagine poverty with a family, so I couldn't get married. For example, it took me some time to accept to

49

have a car; an atheist bought it for us. That was an eye-opener; an atheist gave it to me, but then couldn't the Lord have had something too? But a car is like faith: what's the point of having faith just for faith's sake? A car is for me to go out and meet those people who are waiting for me to love them. When wealth is in the service of poverty it becomes less narrow and lets love squeeze through.

A big Brazilian landowner came up to me after a talk and said: 'Here you are, I give you my estate; do what you want with it for Jesus' sake.' I answered: 'No, I'll do nothing. You are the one who is going to come to the Lord; you, on your land, with all your wealth, are the one who is going to bear witness to the Lord.' Yes, I've changed; absolute poverty as I saw it, didn't fit in with marriage, and so, when love came along I was in trouble. I told Hildegard I would be glad to get married, but that I wanted twenty-five kids (in French, *gosses*), and it wasn't an easy pun to make!

**GÉRARD.** — We are all looking for happiness, and casting things away frightens us all, but then we read: 'Blessed are the poor in spirit, for theirs is the kingdom of heaven' (Matt 5. 3).

I have checked: all translations agree on the verb; it is always in the present. The kingdom of heaven is given straightaway, here, on earth, at this moment.

**HILDEGARD.** — One of the things I especially learnt in the Third World was that the poor are much more vulnerable to the spirit of the Gospel than we are. The word of God enters directly into their lives and transforms it. We are too rich, with our doctrines, our theologies, our theories and our fears. We live inside this fortress and the Gospel message doesn't get through any more. We 'have' technology, we 'have' bombs, we 'have' money, we 'have' the moon, and we 'have' power. We 'have' everything, but nothing to love, which means we are the slaves of all our 'having'. Between everything we 'have' and ourselves there is a fog. We see things as if they were a part of life, of our life, and we want to seize them in order to seize life, but the more we try to grab hold of them the more we are faced with emptiness. The spirit of poverty is a naked, innocent look. You can't possess life without killing it immediately. Vigorous realism with regard to our 'having' has been practiced by all non-violent people, be it Gandhi, Lanza del Vasto, St Francis, Thomas Merton or Cesar Chavez. Relations set up between men who take as their model the one we have with things, that is a 'having' relation, are by that very fact relations of violence. It's called exploitation, oppression or murder; of course, all the nuances and all the subtleties in between make no difference to this basic fact. Being freed from 'having' is being free with regard to things and people, but above all it gives you the strength to free and to respect freedom by helping it to grow. Gandhi fostered freedom in those who listened to him and followed him; Martin Luther King freed the blacks from their fear, from the power of the Whites, and enabled them to hold up their heads. 'Only as long as fear makes each individual tremble inwardly can a system that exploits and excludes the vast majority keep itself going.'[29] The spirit of poverty creates ties based on the characteristics of life and not of death.

Life is change, multiplicity, diversity and liberty: in death everything is reduced to uniformity. No violent government, no violent institution can accept change. Each one of us knows from his own experience how disturbing changes and upheavals are, because they hit us in our 'having', whether it be religious, psychological or economic.

JEAN. — There are no more taboos, racial barriers or class barriers when you let the Spirit of poverty act. All that falls to pieces. Jesus showed that when he spoke to women and treated the Roman and Samaritan enemies with the same love as the Jews. Outsiders, prostitutes and traitors to the people (the publicans) were his 'guests'. 'Morality' got a mighty kick in the teeth, and it is still going on! Commitment to the liberation of man is an essential element in our faith in Christ, the Liberator. Every compromise with the structures that oppress man is a blow against faith itself. The oppressive structures are those which encourage division, which cut men in two: left-right, rich-poor, friend-enemy, etc. And you realize this poison is going to spread, it's going to kill the relations between man, nature and things. It is no accident if men who live in total poverty have an extraordinarily rich relationship with their environment. Ecology without non-violence is a pitiful thing. Basically all these divisions have the same origin in my eyes: the refusal of a loving relationship. For a Christian that's called 'sin'. The love relationship that determines all the others is the one we have with God.

A man and wife who love each other depend each one on the other, and when I say we should re-establish relations of dependence on God, it's that sort of relationship that I mean. It is dishonest to talk of man's dependence on God without saying it is the dependence of love. We must be honest with God; he is not rich, he never wants to possess, but to share. The economic order which reigns in the modern world needs to be transformed radically for it to find both the grounds for its existence and its truth. Perhaps necessity will come to the rescue of our lack of faith.

**GÉRARD.** — Yes, but what about happiness in all that, haven't you forgotten it?

**HILDEGARD.** — Poverty brings you face to face with yourself; it gives you your own being as gift, you find yourself by becoming yourself, and that's where the adventure really starts. Because when you find yourself, you find He who lives within you at the same time. And the happiness He gives you is beyond all words.

**GÉRARD.** — You are teaching us to read the Beatitudes back to front: 'Become poor and you will be happy.' But do you read the last Beatitude the same way? I could sum it up this way: 'If people spit in your face because of me, are you going to find happiness?' With the sort of life you two have led, I should think you must have been knocked about and spat on quite a lot.

JEAN. — The first time I went to be tortured was in 1942. I left the prison camp where I was at the time, accompanied by two armed soldiers in order to go to the fortress nine kilometres away. I was overwhelmed by joy: I was handcuffed and I was praying. It was extraordinary. Hildegard won't tell you this, but I can; she was imprisoned in Brazil with Adolfo Perez Esquivel, the 1980 Nobel Peace Prizewinner. The guards blindfolded them and made them listen to the amplified recordings of cries from tortured prisoners. Two days later the order came to let them go; someone had realized they were foreigners. The guards were ordered to feed them well before letting them out, but they both refused. They said they wanted to fast because they acknowledged that they themselves, just like their guards, were responsible for the injustice in the world; fast in order to free themselves from all resentment towards these same guards and allow their consciences to open up.

Hildegard, I know you will suffer again tonight; the nightmare will come back.

HILDEGARD. — That Beatitude is also the key to understanding the real problems of the oppressed, those who are condemned to live a subhuman life. It teaches us 'identification'. Gandhi shared the life of the untouchables; Danilo Dolci lives with illiterate peasants in Sicily; Cesar Chavez has lived through the negation of dignity the Californian farm workers have to undergo. It's not a question of psychological identification, of 'acting as if'. No. To identify you must give up material riches and social and political privileges. That's nothing new: 'Love thy neighbour as thyself'. That's what identification means. Jesus took it up and developed it: 'Everything you will do even to the least, you will do to me.' In my eyes, the Christians and their churches are part of economic systems geared uniquely to profit, and not to man's real needs. Whether they intend to or not they maintain exploiting structures, based on racial and social discrimination.

Christians believe the Beatitudes. We believe we are sons of God, and would be called upon as such to strive for peace. But we can only become sons of God by working for peace! Gandhi explained his political commitment in this way: 'I couldn't live a religious life without identifying myself with the whole of humanity, and I couldn't do that without getting involved in politics.'[30] We will become sons of God by feeding those who hunger and thirst for justice. We will come to the light by doing what is true.

# IV

GÉRARD. — For you, the source of non-violence has a name: Jesus. He is the 'Pure Non-violent One', you say. No action or word in his life is sullied by violence or by lack of absolute respect for man. Jesus identified himself just as absolutely with man and yet he didn't create a non-violent movement or take part in the liberation of his country from the Roman oppressor! Why didn't he take a political option? You reproach Christ's disciples, Christians and the churches for refusing to commit themselves to paths of action the founder himself never took.

JEAN. — Jesus lived in a country where three currents of force and violence were confronting each other. First of all there were the oppressors, the Roman occupiers, and then the ruling class, especially the Jewish clergy who betrayed holy law: Jesus often reproached them with that. Finally, there were the liberation, or at least resistance movements — the zealots — who based their action on violence. Time has not altered this situation; nowadays you still find it, or something similar, in many Third World countries.

The three groups have a fundamental conviction in common; violence is justified when it defends truth and justice, or when it defends the humiliated. Deep down in their hearts Jesus' companions were of the same opinion, since Peter still used his sword in Gethsemane What was Christ's attitude? He rejected power, the one Satan wanted to offer him, because when you use the sword of power you always serve Satan, whatever your intentions are.

GÉRARD. — René Girard defined Satan as the 'founding mechanism' of violence: 'Satan is one with the circular mechanisms of violence, with the imprisonment of men in cultural or philosophical systems which assure their *modus vivendi* with violence.'[31]

**JEAN.** — Jesus refused to take part in violent movements because their methods killed love and justice, and their goals were not the same as his. But, no doubt, the harsh criticism Jesus heaped on the Jewish political and religious leaders went along with what they got from the zealot revolutionaries. You have the same situation in Latin America, for example; the guerillas' analysis of the situation and their criticism of the violation of the basic rights of man go along with those made by representatives of the non-violent resistance movements, and both are determined to carry on the struggle even if it means sacrificing their own lives. But from the moment someone fighting for liberty uses the same violent methods as the system in power, in order to be more effective, that same system has a greater chance of being reinstated. Jesus rejected it. Jesus was concerned first of all with individuals: he approached every individual who crossed his path with love and truth, and so sowed the seeds of a liberating energy within him. Telling the truth never goes without suffering in a system based on injustice. Jesus severely condemned all kinds of violence: hypocrisy, greed for power and exploitation practiced by political leaders. He denounced the murders committed by those sticklers for the law, the Pharisees. He rejected the death penalty for the woman taken in adultery. It was an attack against the lie, which reigned as prince of the world at that time as it does now. But with all this denunciation, Christ would only have been a courageous revolutionary if, at the same time, he hadn't also been an inexhaustible source of creative love. The transformation of men who still encounter him today, in all corners of the world, is a living proof of this.

Without Jesus I'm a failure; with Him, I am a poor man. Those are the ones, the unschooled, the illiterate, the uneducated, he gives as mission to set the world on fire. The very being of these men is renewed by the Spirit of truth; the very core of their human substance opens up and lets love flow out. You just have to think of Saint Stephen, the first witness of Jesus, and that coward Peter, who threw himself into action. They were freed of fear, passivity and selfishness. That's too brief a summary of the action of Jesus. The non-violent movement which was created from these first friends of Jesus still exists: it's called the 'Church'.

**HILDEGARD.** — It is impossible to sum up Jesus' non-violence; that would be just another theory, another 'scenario for intellectuals' as Jean says. I would just like to outline the forms love takes with Jesus. Jesus took over love for one's neighbour, which was in the Jewish law. He illustrated it with the parable of the Good Samaritan. He showed a heretic, an adversary, who applies the law of love; but he answered the man who recited correctly the commandment 'thou shalt love thy neighbour as thyself' with 'thou art not far from the Kingdom of Heaven'. We sometimes believe that love for one's neighbour is the 'summary' of the Gospel. We are not far off.

Love for one's enemy is one more step towards evangelical non-violence, but it is not the whole story. On the eve of his death, Jesus gave his definition of non-violence: 'Love one another *as* I have loved you.' 'Greater love hath no man than to lay down his life for those he loves.' You can't add anything to that.

It would be a good idea, dear reader, if you stopped reading and shut this book for a moment.

**JEAN.** — Lay down your life! Violent people do exactly the same. Five million dead in the first World War, 40 million in the Second World War and a million in Vietnam. Violent people give their lives, but they also take the lives of others; they make sure their lives are paid for with the lives of others. The non-violent person 'gives' his life. He doesn't 'take' the other's, he 'gives' it for the other.

And when I say 'give one's life' I am not just talking of death, I'm talking of everything that makes up a life, all the love that can be contained in a life.

**GÉRARD.** — I feel I want to hammer on the words, beat them because of their laziness and the way they are so worn. It's become just another cliché: Christ died for us, he gave his life for us. Nobody turns a hair. Ah no! I don't want any of that, it isn't human! Jean, you should understand me as well. Where is his victory? Have you seen it?

**JEAN.** — I can't answer your question, I am absolutely unable to because it is way beyond me. 'And it came to pass that, while they communed together and reasoned, Jesus himself drew near, and went with them. But their eyes were holden that they should not know him. And he said unto them, "what manner of communications are these that you have one to another, as ye walk and are sad?. . . . Certain of them which were with us went to the sepulchre, and found it even as the women had said: but *him* they saw not." . . . And they drew unto the village, whither they went and he made *as though* he would have gone further. But they constrained him, saying, "Abide with us: for it is toward evening, and the day is far spent." And he went in to tarry with them. And it came to pass, as he sat at meat with them, he took bread, and blessed it, and brake, and gave to them. And their eyes were opened, and they knew him; and he vanished out of their sight. And they said one to another, "Did not our heart burn within us, while he talked with us by the way" . . .' (Luke 24. 14–32).

Our life is a long walk, even if we get the impression we are moving away from him. He walks with us. 'The Word has never been uttered for the organization of a particular form of knowledge, but to link up with man's inner word.'[32]

Nobody will walk for you; you will go your own way in your own solitude. Throughout his whole life Jesus showed there is only one way to break free of the shackles of violence: Love. Nobody can love for you. Non-violence makes people exist, and it only exists through men who live love as Jesus lived it.

**GÉRARD.** — Thank you for not giving a theology lesson. The resurrection doesn't touch men's intellect but their hearts, where the source of energy is that enables men to go back over the path they have taken in despair, even if it means we ourselves have to carry the light our surroundings do not give us. The world around us loves classifying and demands categories. Those who are not clearly labelled are kicked out. In order to exist for other people we must be put away in their mental filing systems; that's the only way you can live a quiet life. And that goes just as much for civil as for religious communities. So, if I was questioning you in order to fill out your identity cards I would say:

Name: GOSS Jean. Profession: railwayman, born in Lyon 1912.

Name: MAYR-GOSS Hildegard. Profession: doctor of philosophy, born in Vienna (Austria) 1930.

And now for the trick question: What do I put down for religion?

**JEAN.** — Christian if you like.

**GÉRARD.** — It's not a question of what I like, you must tell the truth.

**JEAN.** — All right, put down 'Catholic'. I was baptized into the Roman Catholic Church. What does 'Catholic' mean?

**GÉRARD.** — It means 'universal'. But it also means you belong to a system that operates with a pope and bishops, and you know better than I do that in that Catholic Church there are not that many people who interpret the Gospel as you and Hildegard do. And can that reference to a religion be combined with the liberty which is the inevitable fruit of non-violence?

JEAN. — For me there is only one Church, which is torn apart. My liberty of life and action doesn't come from a church, but from the discovery of Christ; I take upon myself the risks of that liberty. I am not well thought of in the Vatican, but that doesn't worry me. Hildegard and I were in Rome during the Vatican Council. We contacted three hundred bishops; ten understood, only one really caught fire: Helder Câmara. For me, killing a man is betraying the Gospel in *every* possible case. There is no exception. Some popes and bishops may agree with certain atheists and say the opposite, that's their business. I have other things to do than unravel history in order to see all the faults the different churches have committed against each other. I am there to say 'Love' to everyone. I don't need to create a new church, a church that would at last be free of all filth and non-violent – that's a myth! I am also prepared to be kicked out by the churchmen, the guardians of morality. With atheists the difficulties are no worse, they are of the same kind. Do you think atheism doesn't shut itself up in hermetic systems? Atheists also build up ramparts of words around their convictions, and set themselves up as moral authorities. Like all moral authorities, whatever their origin, they can set enormous strength against whatever might upset their power. They all count on number to impose their wills. Non-violence knows how to do without number in order to count on the Spirit, and that's the way all things can be renewed. Atheists, just like believers, have their 'orthodoxies,' that is their fears, and if non-violence makes me free in my relations with the churches, it makes me just as free in my relations with my atheist brothers. In the prison camp where I began my life of non-violence I had an atheist friend. He was the one who gave me my first lessons in evangelical love, and I was free enough to accept them from him.

**HILDEGARD.** — It's true Jesus didn't found a non-violent movement like those existing in different parts of the world nowadays, and in my opinion that fact is very important. For Jesus we are not just 'agents', but 'friends'. He has given us everything so that we can make his Spirit live in different historical situations. In one way or another Caesar will always be with us in our world, and so it will always be necessary to take on responsibilities and carry out economic, social or political projects. In Poland, our non-violent friends live in an atheistic social organization. They uphold all initiatives that foster human dignity, but are firmly opposed, with all the risks that entails, to all actions by the authorities that go against that fundamental dignity.

In Latin-America, the same non-violent people oppose so-called 'Catholic' governments in the name of human dignity, If, at the time of the Vatican Council only one bishop committed himself body and soul to non-violence, there are now forty in Latin America and Monseigneur Romero has paid the price.

We don't need to worship Caesar. Perhaps the churches are afraid of teaching their faithful disobedience to Caesar because this disobedience could create a movement of liberty that might have repercussions within the church itself.

**JEAN.** — In my eyes, the Church is all those who believe in Jesus Christ, now and in the future. The big problem with the churches is that they are afraid to admit their mistakes and make a public confession. They all talk of peace and human rights, but they all have a theology of the just war and the lesser evil up their sleeves. What a mess! A tiny stone just needs to hit your windscreen, and that's it; you can't see straight any more, everything is distorted and shattered. The lesser evil, the just war, legitimate defence through murder, that's the little stone, and it's your love for others that is shattered.

**GÉRARD.** — Don't institutions need to produce violence in order to survive? And churches or political systems are institutions in some respects, therefore sources of violence. How can a non-violent person live in or with an institution, even if it is a church?

HILDEGARD. — I had to live in the Third World, in Africa and Latin America, in order to really live the Church. There it is no longer a pyramidal structure as we know it, but rather a union of communities. In these communities the Gospel becomes 'Life' because it is no longer filtered by intellectual theories, but goes directly to work on people's hearts. The Gospel read 'with your nose to the text' provokes consciences, brings them to life and helps them act at one and the same time. There is no need to channel these actions in a particular direction or stamp them with a specifically religious mark in order to take possession of them; you just need to uphold them with love. I would like to quote our friend Fragoso, Bishop of Crateus, in the hunger-stricken north-east of Brazil: 'During his peasant life my father was a slave, and I know thousands of peasants who are like him, and I know there are millions in Brazil. These millions of peasants are my brothers. I believe in their dignity. The day I stop struggling for them, the day I stop struggling for them to be men who can stand upright, on that day I shall betray my conscience. And I shall also betray my mission of bishop. Brothers, a man doesn't retreat; Brother farmers, I expect you to be men. A man is not afraid of prison, is not afraid of weapons. You should know that the advancing wave of terrorism aims to stifle the efforts you are making to free yourselves. Do not be afraid, brother farmers. Do not be afraid of anything or of anyone. Be only afraid of hating, of feeling hatred in your hearts. Be afraid of nothing else.'[33]

We only need to follow this radio speech with an extract from the encyclical of Leo XIII to the tertiaries of St. Francis to realize how far we have progressed: 'This problem, finally, for which politicians seek a solution with so much difficulty, of the relation between the rich and the poor, this problem we say, would be completely resolved if it is established and if we persuade ourselves that poverty does not lack greatness, that the rich should be compassionate and generous, and that the poor should be industrious and resigned to their fate. Indeed, neither the one nor the other are born for the transient wealth of this world, but for heaven, which the one should attain by patience and the other by charity.' (encyclical of the 17th September, 1882, given by Leo XIII for the 700th anniversary of the birth of St. Francis).[34]

GÉRARD. — That same encyclical enables us to follow a non-violent 'truth' in its subterranean passages and when it comes to the light.

The pope was speaking to the lay members of the Franciscan brotherhood and said that St Francis 'organized it wisely, less by particular rules than according to the very laws of the Gospel, which certainly would not seem too difficult for any Christian; Obey the commandments of God and the Church, abstain from factions and brawling, not to misappropriate the goods of others; only take up arms for the defence of religion and the country.'[35] Saint Francis with weapons in his hands!

According to a historian of the Franciscan Order, James Mayer O.F.M.,[36] an employee of Emperor Frederick II (grandson of Frederick Barbarossa, nicknamed Stupor Mundi, emperor from 1212 till 1250) complained there were too many tertiaries in the country, and as they refused to carry arms the price for mercenaries was rocketing. St. Francis, when he encountered Christ, discovered absolute respect for man and the non-violence of the first Christian communities. Nowadays thousands of Christians all over the world are sending back their call-up papers and their decorations, and have become conscientious objectors in the name of the Gospel. Truth is stronger than the earth; it keeps coming back, and each time it has a new face. When you go to the Middle East, to Lebanon and Palestine, when you are faced with Orientals, Indians,

Chinese or Japanese, you cannot give truth Jesus' face, and yet you speak to them of non-violence.

**JEAN.** — It only seems difficult, as does the fact that I speak only one language, French, in all countries. You know, the Holy Spirit does exist!

In chapter 42 of the Koran, verses 34–40, it says: 'God destines the treasures of heaven to those who avoid iniquity and crime, silence their anger in order to forgive. To those who, submissive to God, make their prayers, order their actions with prudence and give the indigent a portion of their wealth, to those who repulse the attacks of injustice. Vengeance should be proportional to the insult; but the generous forgiving man has his reward with God who *hates violence.*'

How necessary this insistence on pardon is at the moment in the Arab countries! As it is for all of us. If someone tears my arm off it's no good my tearing both his arms off and the arms of all his family, I'll have my revenge, but I won't get my arm back. I was so attached to my mother that if someone had taken it into his mind to hurt her I would have killed him; but of course that wouldn't have got me my mother back. But if I could have given him my arm, given my arm to the other out of love, that would be more than giving, it would be 'forgiving'. I would love the other one, accepting him in all his being, including his crime against me. He would be free, and so would I. He would no longer fear me and we would be reconciled. I think redemption is something like that.

The following testament of a young Lebanese illustrates this redemptive forgiveness.

*In the name of the Father, the Son and the Holy Spirit,*

*When I began writing this testament it was as if another person was speaking for me. Nowadays everyone is in danger, Lebanese and others living in Lebanon as well. As I am one of them I can see myself being kidnapped and killed on the road from Nabha to my village. And if this intuition turns out to be true I am leaving a word for my family, the people of my village and my country. I say to my mother and my sisters in all assurance: don't be sad, or at least don't weep and don't mourn too much. This absence, in fact, however long it may seem, will be short: we will meet again, that's certain, we'll meet again in heaven, the eternal home; that's where joy is to be found. But don't be afraid, the mercy of God will reunite us all.*

*I have one request to make of you: forgive with all your heart those who have killed me; ask with me that my blood, even if it is the blood of a sinner, may serve as atonement* (fidya) *for the sin of Lebanon; that it be mingled with the blood of all the victims who have fallen, on all sides and of all religious confessions, offered as the price of the face, love and friendship which have disappeared from this country, and even from the whole world. May my death teach men charity; may God console you, watch over you and help you in life. Don't be afraid, I do not regret this world at all. One thing grieves me, that you will be sad. Pray, pray and pray, and love your enemies.*

*And I say to my country: 'Those who dwell in a house can have different opinions; they don't hate each other, they can get angry with each other, but without becoming enemies; they can quarrel, but without killing each other'.*

*Remember the days of friendship and charity; forget those of anger and discord. We have eaten, drunk and worked together; we have lifted up our prayer to the one God together; we must die together. My father had a metuali (Shiite) as a partner, whom I called 'Uncle Hussein'; I liked to call him that. They were partners for seventy five years, without breaking their contract or keeping accounts. Remember, it often happens that you can't borrow a hundred pounds from your own brother, and you just have to go and find someone in the village, be he Shiite, Maronite, Sunnite or Druze, and he will help you out. That's something everyone knows, but sin blinds us to it. Each one should come back to prayer according to his belief and his conscience, so that God can wipe out anger and that the plans of the mighty may be reduced to* dust on the soil of this land, which is not obliged to pay in blood for their machinations.

In heaven I shall not be at rest as long as this situation lasts in Lebanon.

You must make my funeral a day of ordination, not a day of mourning and sadness.

For my burial, can Father Boutros celebrate mass, without large numbers of priests or any official announcement. And if Abou-Khalil could make my coffin from a few old boxes, that would suit me perfectly. No funeral meal — I hope people will forgive me for that — and no shooting; I am indeed but dust; but the Force of God is going to let me share in the divine life. 'That is how it must be done'.

People are going to talk, but that should be of no importance for you. If only they had a little pity they wouldn't kill each other, and wouldn't let the wolves be better than us. What a mistake they are making!

Let the choir sing as much as they wish: that will please me.

As I am writing I am thinking of everyone, without forgetting anyone: my comrades and my friends. My affection for them would like to find words of hope; I think I have found the word that will do: 'Let them pray for me, fear God and love Him'. In your prayers always spare a thought for the monks and the nuns, living witnesses of Christ among us here on earth: especially the Franciscans, the Jesuits and the Fathers of the Prado; through them was I able to know God, not to mention the material help they have given me.

As for myself, I am above all only a sinner.

I ask forgiveness of everyone, for I am a sinner towards everyone.

Courage!

I a sinner, in our Saviour Jesus Christ.


Copy written on the 27.12.75 at the Notre-Dame-de Jamhour College,

Beirut (Lebanon)

Ghassibé Kayrouth, twenty-two-years old, was killed as he foresaw in this testament found in his room.

**GÉRARD.** — The city of peace, Jerusalem, has become the symbol of war, of the butchery between Israel and Ismael, the two sons of Abraham. You go to that country very often. How do you talk about non-violence to men who are impregnated with the God of the Old Testament, the God of Deuteronomy who says: 'But of the cities of these people which the Lord thy God doth give thee for an inheritance, thou shalt save alive nothing that breatheth' (Deut. 20. 16).

**JEAN.** — I don't read the Bible like that. What is God getting at, with the Jews and with us? At this: 'Thou shalt love they neighbour as thyself'. That is God's goal, God's thinking. The rest is just intellectual problems. At the moment in the Middle East, if moslems, jews and christians didn't live non-violence every day – and I repeat every day – there would be nothing left but corpses. If people lose their land, what happens to them? If the French were scattered all over the world there would be no more France. Israel has survived because they lived in the shadow of the law. A country needs defenders, the Law of God needs witnesses, and I think there were innumerable 'witnesses' to the Jewish Law in the ghettoes and the prison camps. I have a feeling of brotherhood with the Jews who, through blood and mire always carried their 'beloved burden'; 'And thou shalt love the Lord with all thy heart' (Deut. 6.5). Non-violence is something you move with.

**HILDEGARD.** — Africans, no doubt because of their inborn respect for life, discovered non-violence and its value without us. If we hear of only violent actions in African countries, that's because only we Europeans instigated and supported such actions on behalf of certain people.

Albert Luthuli, Nobel Peace Prizewinner in 1961, had

only one weapon in his struggle: non-violence. In 1952 he had been elected president of the African National Congress. In non-violent struggles Africans, and especially, perhaps, African women, regained their pride and their dignity of being. Apartheid is still a leprous sore, but some Whites also come and fight against this disease, alongside the Blacks. The non-violence of the Blacks is a challenge to the 'white' churches and has set them on the road to deepening the evangelical values. And yet the Dutch Reformed Church still maintains its racist position and theology. Luthuli was arrested, put under house-arrest, and died after many years of imprisonment. I have met his daughter: she is continuing the non-violent struggle among her people. Julius K. Nyerere, ex-president of Tanzania, has created a 'typically African socialist movement based on the family in the African sense of the word. It is opposed to capitalism in order to build a happy society; it is also opposed to doctrinaire socialism which tries to construct a perfect society on a philosophy which states that struggle between man and man is inevitable'.[37]

*Ujamaa* is a Swahili term meaning 'spirit of community', and the entire economical and social structure of the country refers to this notion.

Ujamaa villages had been founded throughout the country by volunteers who had all their goods in common. The political and administrative heads were not there just to transmit orders down from the top of the pyramid, but to discuss and take part. We find there an absolute rejection of any totalitarian leanings, the personality cult or dictatorship. In my opinion the Africans are finding, through their own culture, what the first Christians lived; they challenge capitalism in all its forms just as much as marxist socialism, because they both oppress men.

All these struggles and projects may not be without their failures and setbacks, but that doesn't mean the truth about man is prevented from growing.

**GÉRARD.** — The oriental 'mystics' have invaded our world and all we have been able to do is find just a slightly different way from our own of satisfying our spiritual needs. Yoga has been purged of its supposedly spiritual aspect and is reduced to a sort of gymnastics; once more we cut off the Source in order to be sure of dying of thirst. Karma Yoga teaches that 'you shall not acquire your personal satisfaction at the price of someone else's suffering', and the same work says, 'It is no real progress to replace the exploited of yesterday by the exploiters of today, if exploitation still exists. It is the exploiters who should accomplish the revolution, for exploitation does not degrade those who are subject to it, but rather those who practice it. It is not the pity felt by the sufferings of the exploited that should appal us, but the moral degradation of the exploiter.'[38]

I quote this passage in preference to other more famous ones from the Gita because it shows what you have experienced through all your encounters; non-violent wisdom is present in the hearts of all men worthy of the name, whatever their race or culture. You speak directly to those who have been impregnated by this wisdom, but is it the same for those who have been cut off from these deep sources?


**JEAN.** — I discovered non-violence in the trade union movement, but don't imagine men waited for Jean Goss in order to discover that the only thing of value in the world was man. The humanists said it before me: 'Non-violence,' said Gandhi, 'is as old as the hills.' Mo Tsu, in China (800 B.C.) declared: 'To kill a man for the good of the world is not doing good for the world. But what is good is to offer oneself as a sacrifice for the world.'[39]

The American writer Henry David Thoreau (1817–1862) discovered 'civil disobedience', and wrote a book about it which inspired Gandhi and Martin Luther King. In Sicily since 1952, Danilo Dolci has been carrying on a non-violent struggle to help the inhabitants of the region become total Italian citizens. His struggle has no religious basis. The value of man is enough to uphold his struggle, and nourish a life devoted to the service of the rejected.

**HILDEGARD.** — We should certainly quote several non-violent initiatives which have no confessional reference. One of the best known is Amnesty International, founded by Peter Benenson and Sean MacBride in 1961. This organization fights for freedom of conscience in the whole world, and uses only non-violent methods: making individuals aware of what is going on, letters to the responsible authorities, etc. Well over ten thousand prisoners have been released. Dictators, like Bokassa, have lost their throne and their deadly effectiveness because Amnesty has had the courage to denounce them.

This organization is not interested in whatever the opinion may be for which a man is condemned. It only wants to know the man. Our friend, Nobel Peace Prizewinner in 1980, Adolfo Perez Esquivel, was an adopted prisoner of Amnesty International when he was imprisoned without judgement and tortured.

What atheism brings to non-violence is positive because it obliges believers to be more rigorous in their attitudes and to seek more depth in their motivations. Atheism and the great monotheist religions have this in common: they have no time for idols, and we create idols every day. We are always ready to grovel before our latest false god. We have even made an idol of man himself. 'Atheism, like the mystics and the saints, though in a different way, helps to purify the image of God.'[40]

In my life, God has not always had the same face, the same image. Different ages, events and struggles, the changing conditions of my life, have transformed my faith and my vision of God. I feel I have been 'on the road' all my life, in a permanent approximation of that living Love, which is God. And I hope I shall always be on this road, making new discoveries. I was baptized into the Catholic Church as a child, and brought up by my parents in a faith founded essentially on the Gospel, and on the dignity and responsibility which flow from it. I met Protestant and Orthodox Christians when I was very young, and we found ourselves united in a single family, bearing witness to respect for the human individual and love for one's enemy in the face of Hitler's regime.

I felt the richness of their faith complemented our Catholic faith, either in their interpretation of the Word, or in the importance they gave to the working of the Spirit of God in the Church. For me, in the face of our atheistic, materialistic civilization, there is one essential task: to bring us all together, to unite us all one day in order to testify together to the non-violence of Christ. To unite ourselves means, in my eyes, to accept the reality of one single Christian church, whose collegial life is rich in varied expressions of our common faith. But, since my youth, my faith has always been critical, towards myself and my own betrayals as much as towards the betrayals of my Catholic church and other Christian churches. This constructive, loving criticism, albeit sometimes severe, has as its yardstick our fidelity to the Gospel, and to the image in which we were created: the Trinity, that non-violent community. Where the Christian churches betray this liberating non-violence of Christ, in their teaching, their life and their structures, they fall back again into the pattern of domination: violence against non-violence. That is where I have to tell the *truth* as God has made me understand it, even if that sets me against old traditions or policies of church leaders. I believe God manifests himself through every believer and non-believer, and the permanent renewal of the Church can only be accomplished through that community of God to which we all belong.


ANNEXE I

Letter from the wife of Adolfo Perez Esquivel to Hildegard and Jean Goss, on the 17th November, 1980

*Dear Hildgard and Jean*          *Buenos Aires, 17–11–80*

*Your last letter moved us deeply. Since then, the news of*

the Nobel Peace Prize award has arrived, which has quite overjoyed us.

On this occasion we think of you a great deal, of your family and all the work you have done for peace. This prize should be celebrated together with all those who have been engaged for years in the difficult task of uniting and reconciling brothers. Even though I have never told you, you should know that through your letters and personal contacts you have stimulated the path Adolfo has taken, in all sorts of ways. He has always considered you to be his first masters who, one day, a long time ago, arrived in Buenos Aires, contacted the Ark and explained very simply and humbly what non-violence was. Do you remember? And since then we have taken the same road together. You have incessantly proposed, informed and taught the way to work and organize ourselves.

You have always accompanied us. In the good times and the bad. That is why I think that you also are the winners of this prize.

Fraternally a big abraço

*Amanda*

# V

**GÉRARD.** — Jesus is dead. For us Christ is a dead man. In no way can he live with us what we live. I say this because this failure permeates our hearts and our minds, and makes us accept the fatality of violence or evil even if we have lost all our red blood cells.

'The poor will always be with you', 'There will always be wars', so what's the point in getting worked up? You know beforehand your effectiveness will be zero. Christ is dead. He is shut up in the tomb of theories and the golden tomb of religions. That's how it is! If he was alive it would show, wouldn't it?

**HILDEGARD.** — The effectiveness of non-violence is as unexpected as the way God or Love bursts into a man's life. On the effectiveness of non-violence depends the survival of all mankind today. If men can't manage to settle their conflicts other than through violence, the power triggered off by the accumulation of our violence will destroy all life on our planet. We have reached a point of no return in the history of man. We haven't got enough clarity of insight into the terrifying madness we accept under the name of balance of terror, but we must also realize that there are not many people in favour of triggering off the nuclear terror. In my opinion, the question of the effectiveness of non-violence is vital for the whole of humanity. If non-violence is not effective the apocalypse is for today.

**JEAN.** — To appreciate the effectiveness of a medicine you need two things: to be aware something is lacking in our organism, that is, to be ill, and second, to realize that the medicine we are using is really active. People who don't want to see violence, and those who don't suffer from violence have no reason to try non-violent solutions.

Those who feel concerned by an injustice, but only want to find a way out of it by counter-violence are unable to judge the effectiveness of non-violence too. We live under the tenacious illusion that violence is effective, that is, that it gives a radical solution to all our problems. We seek peace while making war, and each war gives birth to the next. No sooner do we finish a hot war than we start up a cold war. The logic of violence is implacable; from one murder you make another. The cross is not the failure of Christ, but the failure of violence.

GÉRARD. — When I discovered non-violence through contact with you, I also discovered that our faculties, in particular our imagination, were riveted to violence. The one could not function without the other.

Every time violence takes a step forward, it immediately draws the imagination with it. The more our violence spreads over the surface of the planet, the more prodigious it becomes in its ingenuity and its refinement, but also in its greed for intellectual, psychic, material and human energy. As long as we don't divorce ourselves from violence we will remain bound to it in all our activities.

JEAN. — That's exactly how the concept of the lesser evil is born. It is better to starve fifty million people to death, as we did in 1980, rather than have a nuclear war. It is better to kill forty million young men than let Hitler live. It is better to accumulate weapons than use them. It's an infernal, vicious circle.

Non-violence is the definitive break in this crazy spiral. Non-violent actions can never adopt the methods of violent action; they would head ineluctably for the same goals as violence: the destruction of man, death and evil.

The source of non-violent action should be clear, otherwise its effectiveness will be clouded. Actions contaminated by the 'lesser evil' become estranged from love, and evolve inescapably towards violence, just the same as violent actions. They can not be effective, that is, bring about the liberation of those who perform them and those who receive them.

Some non-violent actions can be interpreted as violent even though they are perfectly clear. A demonstration can be interpreted as violent by those who have to put up with it from behind their windows. In reality it's an attack on sleeping consciences. If you wake somebody up in the middle of the night because their house is on fire it is perceived by the sleeper as a 'violence'. If you tell people: 'We are suffocating under injustice; your passivity is killing innocent men and women!', is that violence? If you shout into deaf ears that our world is dying of lies, lust for power and armed butchery, is that violence? Effectiveness is also undermined by violence. Something is effective if it reassures immediately. When violence increases, in the name of effectiveness we increase the number of police, that is to say, the repression; and so we are safe. Now studies have shown[41] that drops in violence correspond to periods when individuals are respected as human beings, and not during periods of police repression. Non-violence has no other goal than to make all men 'truly human'.

To say you mustn't attack violence under the pretext that it can't be eradicated, that it will always make us go to war, that there will always be oppressors and oppressed, is as if you called all doctors idiots because they try to snatch condemned men from the jaws of death. We will all have to die one day, so what's the use of dragging it out? You might just as well kill men while they are still fit — that's what those who organize wars think.

HILDEGARD. — Very often non-violent people are reproached for having never prevented a war from breaking out, or a massacre from taking place. It's true, but that is not the fault of non-violence. We have been cultivating violence for years, letting social, economic and political injustices go from bad to worse, and then we have spread this cancer onto other continents. Hitler wasn't born the day he made the concentration camps. The second volume of *Mein Kampf* came out in 1927; everything was in it. A non-violent man, Bart de Ligt, threw himself against this rising wave of insane violence; he organized the 'mobilization against all wars' with his movement, the War Resisters' International.[42] He showed how all European countries were intoxicated by violence. He quoted this: 'Only war can allow man to display his most sublime forces.'[43]

In France, *Paris-Soir* quoted the Mussolini declaration: 'Every man should keep his share of barbarity. We must be hard.' In the *Echo de Paris*, Mussolini is acclaimed: 'You are great. You are wise at last, for you believe only in the virtue of bayonets. You prepare to defend peace with cannons.' *Le Journal* noted that when he glorified militarism 'the Duce has only exalted an ideal which is common to all nations in the world'.[44]

Of course, these are only small examples, and yet their message is clear; the work of the non-violent people, to remove the dust from their fellow-citizens' eyes, was done. What the non-violent people saw turned out, unfortunately, to be right.

Sometimes risking their own lives, they had denounced the mirages the rulers were making with our suffering. An international effort had put forward solutions. The non-violent people offered medicine to a sick man who thought he was in perfect health. Today we are in a similar situation, but we have moved up a step in violence. Who listens to non-violent people? Those who will be the victims of the next and last of all wars? No! The only people who listen to them are the leaders — in order to put them in prison because they upset their plans. Today, in France, to say that you refuse to kill is an offence which could lead you to prison. Why don't we want to look these murderous realities in the face? Why can we do no more than fatalistically shrug our shoulders? If we don't want violence to overrun the whole planet, we must begin by rooting it out at home, in our own selves. The violence of each of us is our beam; we can see nothing as long as we accept it in front of our eyes. We can see nothing but 'violence', since everything will be perceived through it. Take the beam away, and non-violence will become effective. During the Second World War, Hitler wanted to force the Danish Jews to wear the yellow star, as he had imposed it in the other occupied countries. King Christian X decided that he also would wear this sign that had become so infamous. The Nazis gave this measure up, and the Jewish community (6,000 people) was spared. The king had eradicated all racism in himself. A man was a man; this enabled him to take effective action. You can imagine what the effect would have been on the world if the French Catholics, with the clergy at their head, had stuck the star of David on themselves. Wasn't it a pope who said that Christians were Semites? Because he had dared oppose Hitler, King Christian X was treated as a prisoner until the German capitulation.

**GÉRARD.** — I know before I ask it that my question is going to make Jean hopping mad. Too bad for me! When we have tried everything, really everything, given lectures, prayed even, and all that has had no result, haven't we got the right to choose violence?

**JEAN.** — I have no authorization to give to anybody. But I have forty years' experience that authorizes me to tell you that you never, and I mean never, do as you say. You do the opposite. You begin with violence, and then you end up looking for non-violent solutions. You want to serve two masters at the same time, to see who pays the better. You practice non-violence reluctantly, like the fellow who gets married with a notice of divorce in his pocket, just in case it doesn't work. Caiaphas said: 'Ye know nothing at all, nor consider that it is expedient for us that one man should die for the people, and that the whole nation perish not' (John 11. 49–50).

People who have recourse to torture use this excuse. The lesser evil just doesn't exist — there's just evil. The effectiveness of non-violence depends on the values it incarnates. I have to live, to bear witness by my life that the only thing of value in life is man, and I have to testify to this value at the risk of my 'own' life. I say testify, and not teach, convert others or anything like that.

When I betray this truth I say: 'I have betrayed,' but I'll never say it's a lesser evil, and that anyway in certain cases you can't do otherwise, or any of that sort of rubbish.

Gandhi said: 'The many failures we have noticed come not from the law (of non-violence) but from those who apply it'.[45] The intellectuals have made me suffer with their theories; the poor I have met in the Middle East countries, or in Latin America have a completely different approach. In those countries the poor practice non-violence simply to survive; they don't feel the need to make it into a theory. In Latin America the slightest act of violence by a peasant signs his arrest warrant, and that guarantees he will be tortured. So they find a way of acting that is no longer violent.

Hildegard and I have always been surprised to see that as the methods used in the struggle became more and more infused with truth and love, the force of non-violence grew prodigiously. We have seen the opposite as well, unfortunately!

If the peasants of the Larzac plateau in southern France had used violent means to defend their land, people would have stopped talking about them a long time ago. But these peasants from the Aveyron department have discovered through their action that 'wheat creates life and weapons kill it'. Their harvest festival collects money for the hungry Third World. The struggle has been going on since 1970, and it has opened up the conscience of thousands of people.

What would be left of the Czechoslovak army and people if they had taken up arms against their Soviet 'friends' in 1968? A whole nation refuses to use violence, and the army will stay in the barracks. The Marxists discovered it without our help: violence doesn't pay. According to a non-Christian Czech friend, two things were missing in Czechoslovak non-violence: love for one's enemies and forgiveness. Perhaps it is up to the Christians to add these two pillars to non-violence to make it effective on all levels, to make it universally effective.

**GÉRARD.** — The facts you quote to show the effectiveness of non-violence are small if we look at them through the eyes of history, in comparison with those 'enormities', military and economic wars. It works for small events, but there are so many where it doesn't work! The historians leave you a few crumbs in order not to plunge you into despair.

**HILDEGARD.** — That's true, they seem 'small' if we stay within the logic of violence. To save six thousand Jews is nothing in comparison with the six million the Germans killed, and it's not much in comparison with the 135,000 dead in the bombardment of Dresden in 1945. It is abominable when the Red Brigades kill in Italy. Mao killed millions of Chinese for his revolution, and that was a 'small' event.[46] The life and death of Jesus Christ was an event of no importance, but who is still living today on the 'divinity' of Augustus Caesar?

Our whole memory is infected with violence; the history we learn at school is the history of our violence, and our 'heroes' are the most violent of them all.

We want to mechanically transpose effectiveness from violence to non-violence. An atomic bomb is capable of killing 'X' million people; what do you set against that? I set against it the human beings who have faith in man. The Soviet Union is not at all frightened by our bombs, but locks up abstract painters and people who confess faith in another god than Marx, Lenin or the late Stalin. Solzhenitsyn, who knows the Soviet strength very well, reproaches the West not for its military weakness, but for its spiritual abdication.

What is an 'important' fact in the eyes of historians? It's a fact that has cost a lot of dead and lots of destruction. That's why children, from their very earliest years, learn to judge the importance of historical events by the height of the piles of corpses. The important event of the Middle Ages was not the Crusades; in reality it was St Francis. Just compare: what remains of Louis XIV that is really living, and what remains of St. Vincent de Paul?

**JEAN.** — If we go on working in the upper reaches of diplomacy we will forget that the basis of non-violence allows us to live a family life every day without murder. 'Be ready to forgive at every moment,' says the rule of Taizé; and in the vast majority of families the world over love and forgiveness allow us to resolve conflicts without bloodshed. Perhaps that is where we can truly measure the demands of non-violence and its effectiveness.

When lies start digging their way into a family, happiness falls to pieces in no time at all. When the cohesion of a couple is based on money, on 'having' instead of being based on love, where is joy?

When our own happiness is threatened or destroyed we suffer. But why shouldn't what is true in family life be equally true for the whole group, for all men?

In the life of a couple, generally speaking, love carries us along at first, and then we are the ones who have to carry love. When we commit ourselves to a human being, be it in marriage or in a group, we commit ourselves to part of humanity just as it is; we must learn to love that part of humanity, just as it is. God loves us just as we are. It gives a person prodigious strength to know that he or she is loved just as he or she is, and I should know. I have been completely crazy with joy for forty years because I know God loves *me*, God loves *us all*.

When I see what present-day diplomacy is preparing for us, I plunge into that love again, and once more I am crazy with happiness.

**GÉRARD.** — For every question we are faced with, either in every day life, or in the life of society in general, there are two ways of reacting. The first, the natural way, is that of violence; the second is that of non-violence.

To choose a path that goes nicely between the two is

impossible, you say. You can not choose life and death in the same breath. In our world this choice is being cut down dangerously; non-violence advances at a snail's pace, and will soon be overtaken. Will we start talking about non-violence when we start fighting with slings and stones again?

**JEAN.** — I met the present pope when he was in Cracov. In half an hour I set out evangelical non-violence to him, and he replied: 'But you're talking to me about the next Council, about Vatican III!' That's right! The Gospel is not for straight away. And then I read in his speech to Unesco: 'How can we be sure that the use of nuclear weapons, even if used in national defence only, or in limited conflicts, will not bring about an inevitable escalation, leading to a destruction that humanity will never be able either to imagine or to accept?'[47]

I'm absolutely flabbergasted. We've come back to the 'just war'. We mix up nuclear war with a cowboy shoot-out, with the goodies on one side and the baddies on the other, and bang! Up goes the whole planet!

But that's my temperament, I'm too impatient. Every minute of hatred, every minute of violence, is a minute of happiness lost. And yet the same John-Paul II, speaking to the workers, said this: 'Our present-day world sees the terrible threat grow, of each side destroying the other, especially with the accumulation of nuclear weapons. The cost of these weapons, and the menacing climate they create, have meant that millions of men, and whole nations, have been deprived of the possibility of eating bread and being free ... The great society of workers should ask, categorically and clearly: where, in which field, and why have the limits to the noble struggle for justice, the struggle for man's well-being, been passed?'[48] And then a bit further: 'Christians can not and do not wish to prepare this world of truth and justice in hatred, but only in the vivifying power of love.'[49] The patience of God is incredible. And yet ...

Non-violence is a germinating seed, and you see nothing

for a long time. I cry in the desert, and see nothing move. To impose non-violence is literally nonsensical. Men take time to be converted, that is to say, to take the path of love.

**HILDEGARD.** — Impatience is one of the characteristics of our time. We are no longer tied to the rhythm of the earth. We want success straight away, and a lot of politicians want to transform men just as they transform machines, by exerting pressures. They impose forms and structures from the outside, which have been neither developed nor set up in common. All dictatorships, whatever their colour, impose 'happiness' on men without asking their opinion. What is imposed is violent, what is violent can only survive through violence. Revolutionary impatience which urges the violent realization of its goals is immature behaviour, foreign to man, to his needs and to the real, true work of liberation. At the same time, it would be a tragic mistake to take that as a pretext for a passive attitude to injustice.

**GÉRARD.** — The 'liberties' and 'happinesses' that are imposed on us always end up getting distorted somewhere; that's true when we are talking about nations, just as it is when we're talking about education. Non-violence reaches into every nook and cranny of life. Sexuality is bound to violence, too, and that great source of anxiety for Western people, the belly and everything that goes into it, has direct repercussions on our behaviour, be it violent or loving.

**JEAN.** — I think if men turn their attention to their stomachs nowadays it's because their souls, their hearts and even their conscience has been emptied. Life has been regulated like a menu; not too much of this in order to avoid cholesterol, a little bit of that for the triglycerids, etc. While we become well-behaved citizens we don't worry so much about what those who govern us are up to. We worry about our own navel while other people are starved. We must talk about this food question, in order to understand that much more clearly just what fasting is, that non-violent manifestation which has such unlimited power. 'To fast,' says the dictionary, 'is to eat less than you need, or not at all.' A hunger-strike then would be apparently only the same as a fast. Danilo Dolci fasted with more than one thousand men (poor Sicilians in all senses of the word) and gave the press the following communiqué: 'Friends of Partinico, the outlaws of Partinico wish to become Italian citizens, members of a truly civilized society. By fasting together on Monday we have purified ourselves before devoting Thursday to the celebration of work. Nobody can prevent us from working together in order and in discipline.'[50]

On the 14th February 1969, Cesar Chavez[51] undertook a fast which lasted till the 10th March. On that day there was a day of thanksgiving attended by ten thousand people, including Senator Robert Kennedy.

Cesar Chavez wrote: 'I am not fasting out of anger for the landowners . . . Our goal is not to destroy the company bosses. We only claim the ability to organize our union and to work in a non-violent manner, so that the farm-workers of our country may live a new day of hope and justice.

'I repeat the principles of this fast: if the establishment of our union should demand the destruction of a single human life, be it that of a landowner, a farm worker or a child, I prefer not to see the union created.'

At Delano on the 29th July 1970, the last of the twenty six company bosses signed the recognition of the union of farm-workers and accepted the collective agreement.

On the 28th December 1977, four tin-miners' wives from Siglo Viente, in Bolivia, started a fast in premises belonging to the archbishopric of La Paz. On the 18th January, the State was obliged to grant the general amnesty these women demanded. Non-violence is not just for men; it is for everyone who becomes aware of his or her own humanity.

'We have risen against man's inhumanity to man. And

that is the combat which gives meaning to our life and nobility to our death,' says Chavez.

**GÉRARD.** — Externally there is little difference between a hunger-strike, whose aim is to extort the satisfaction of certain demands, a political hunger-strike which is a sort of protest, and the true fast. Deep down what changes is the view of man. A hunger-strike is a calorie-strike. Fasting is purifying the body, raising the level of the struggle to the human dimension. If the body is a bag of meat that runs on calories like a steam engine, fasting becomes absurd; at best a sort of oil change. Not far off is the danger of people trying to outbid each other: I've done thirty days more than the other fellow. Fasting is simply not eating. 'The most intimate relation one has with oneself is eating.'[52] And we eat because we are men; animals feed themselves. That is often the only 'liturgy' left to us, along with that of the sports grounds.

Fasting is a total commitment to non-violence. Non-violent commitments are not spiritual or metaphysical; they are 'corporal'. A man should be present in his entirety so that he becomes an 'incarnation' of non-violence; it is impossible to be non-violent by proxy.

**HILDEGARD.** — If that was possible we wouldn't be travelling all the time. The fast we have rediscovered in non-violence is also the fast of the great human traditions: Buddhism, Hinduism, Islam, Judaism and Christianity. They are all familiar with purification through fasting, and its liberating effects.

**GÉRARD.** — Once more we come across 'purification' and 'liberation'. These religious overtones could make people ill at ease. In our world, when you need to be purified or liberated, you take some medicine, and that's it, it's finished. Fasting seems to be some sort of magical rite, comparable to the redskins; war paint and amulets.

**HILDEGARD.** — Fasting is not an act of moral magic.

You fast to free yourself from your illusions and to purify your thoughts and your actions of your own malice.

Our illusions are legion: our existence based uniquely on having. Having food, having a name, having a reputation; 'Me.' 'Me'. 'Me'. Fasting separates what was originally laid down by love in our actions from the personal dross which does not belong to it. Fasting binds us to others because it takes us down to our own personal nakedness. 'Since Jesus Christ, no other space but human flesh unites the cosmos. Body-consciousness, and not head consciousness, is the seat of faith, hope and love.'[53]

**GÉRARD.** — The person who throws himself or herself into the non-violent experience discovers that he or she is really a human being; they commit themselves totally, and, groping through a mist perhaps, discover true greatness, real existence, oneness. Saint Ephrem the Syrian (306–373) said that duality was the source of violence.[54] If there is body and soul, one mortal, the other immortal, you can always kill what is anyway only mortal, can't you? Fasting puts things back as they should be; it makes us experience our oneness and our participation in creation.

# VI

JEAN. — What is essential to non-violent action is not the form of the struggle, but the mentality, the spirit, the attitude that inspires it. The means of action is only the visible manifestation of the dynamics behind non-violence. The non-violent power of fasting is prodigious. Gandhi, one man all by himself, because he fasted, obtained a reform of the caste system which oppressed the untouchables (1932); one man against a tradition going back thousands of years, considerable vested interests and an occupying government.

That is characteristic of non-violent actions: the number of people involved is often ridiculously small. In reality, what happens is that man's true strength, the faith of love, is released; when it begins to act, it moves mountains.

GÉRARD. — You have twisted the neck of a problem that upsets a lot of us. For some we must change unjust, therefore violent, structures; for others we must change ourselves, since 'the rest will be added unto you'. Must we act before or after contemplating? These are intellectual questions, aren't they, Jean?

JEAN. — And how! One day I was talking to a Russian, and he made this remark: 'We Communists are atheists, and we know it; but you Christians are as well, and you don't know it.'

That's true. But the Russians think they are Communists and they aren't. That means, in my opinion, that we set up or change structures not according to what we think we are, but according to what we are.

We think we are 'Christians' and we accept armaments.

We think we are Socialists and we prepare the death of the working class the world over. The structures show us, as in a mirror, what we are, and not what we think. Look closely. It's very instructive. The violence in a structure measures very exactly the gap between our intellectual talk and our deep self.

With men who are what they think, action moves immediately in the direction of truth, justice and love. Things move all round them. When you approach men of that sort you wake up, you start living.

**GÉRARD.** — Non-violence is not for everyone, then. It just concerns a few enlightened people who, once they are dead, bury non-violence along with their own selves. What has become of Martin Luther King's movement since his death? What has become of India since Gandhi's death?

**JEAN.** — Who is love reserved for? For heroes? For educated people? Have you ever seen love die? People we love die, and for a time we get the impression love has deserted our world; but their love lives in us and through us. It carries on, but with another face. 'Except the grain of seed dies it cannot bear fruit'. Violence doesn't die with violent people, either, unfortunately.

'Murderous violence, skilfully organized, is nowadays the sorry prerogative of the human race.'[55] But the love of God is greater than our violence; it is what gives man his value, even if he is unable to grasp its breadth and its source. Man is blind by birth, like the one that the Gospel according to Saint John speaks of, and very often all we are interested in is dissecting his guilt and arguing about whether or not he fits into our mental categories and our cultural superstructures. In him, in this blind man, in all men, the works of God must manifest themselves. And what are the works of God? Love. If that's true we mustn't waste time, we must get down to work while we still have time. The glory of God, said Saint Ireneus, is living man, man living in fulness. The glory of God is not the man with the amputated heart, the man incapable of love or the man starved of tenderness.

Are we ashamed to love and to let ourselves be loved? When I talk of bombs everyone says I am a realist; if I talk of love, people look at me in a strange way: 'Ah, Jean's going off into his utopia', they seem to say. Just imagine a mason in the 13th century if you talked to him about Social Security, Family Allowances and Unemployment Benefit. Utopia!

We can see the acceleration of history in the speed of rockets going to the moon. You can also see it in social achievements. The cathedrals are magnificent, but Social Security is Gospel.

**HILDEGARD.** — Everyone, even violent people, can live non-violence. From the 14th June till the 1st October 1976, the prisoners in Louvain central prison in Belgium were engaged in a non-violent struggle. Men who had been locked up because of their violence, three hundred men deprived of their liberty because they had committed crimes, had been able to act as true men. This fact is astonishing. It shows that men considered to be second-class citizens can regain their dignity and free themselves from their own violence.

A number of measures were granted which enabled these men to set out once again on the path leading to their own humanity.[56]

**GÉRARD.** — Aren't you a bit too optimistic some days? At the moment violence is getting fatter and fatter. I'm thinking of the murderous violence in the Third World and among the poor of the wealthy nations, because economic laws are as pitiless as bombs. There is also the petty violence which slowly and insidiously fills up our daily lives. It is as if we were vaccinated against these two sorts of violence. We don't even notice them any more; we just live with them. J. Léauté[57] explains that violent crime is only a very small fraction of crime in general, and an even smaller part of violence. The latter manifests itself in the way it has grown considerably among non-delin-quents. It creeps into the relations between ordinary, honest folk. It becomes our violence. Studies have shown that the solitude of modern man, particularly in cities, plays a large part in the growth of violence. Large housing estates and administrative indifference make men uniform, and by this very fact make them indifferent to each other; they no longer exist as humans, and violence is often a way of communicating in despair, a cry of absurdity.

**HILDEGARD.** — Generally speaking, the first non-viol-ent action is not fasting, but dialogue. The other side, the adversary, is recognized as a man, he is taken out of his anonymity and exists in his own right, for what he really is, a man. To engage someone in a dialogue is to recognize him, have faith in him. At every step in the non-violent struggle, at every level we try tirelessly to establish a dia-logue, or re-establish it if it has broken down. When I say 'the other side', that could be a group of men or a government.

You must admit that the sort of 'dialogue' established according to Stalin's method still has a large following.

How many divisions has the Pope? Tell me how great your power is, what degree your potential for violence is, so that I may see if I can condescend to having a dialogue with you. Engage in a dialogue with the people of the Third World? Why? They have nothing. It's obvious that the bases of the sort of dialogue we are talking about are exactly the opposite to that way of thinking. We must above all get through to what is true in our adversary.

When we recognize the adversary's individuality the first point in a dialogue, we break down the wall of prejudices; we endeavour to create, in a human and objective way, a point of departure for a real exchange of opinions.

**JEAN.** — In reality we never go about things like that. We bombard the person we are speaking to with our truths and our reproaches, and we don't leave him a shred of anything positive. At all costs we set up a separation between him and us. He is the enemy, and so evil, and I, well I'm the one who is good, so in the right. We cut the world in two, but we steer clear of cutting into our own hearts.

In 1964 we went to live for a whole year in Brazil with Myriam and Etienne, our children. It wasn't the very best of times to go. Some friends warned us: 'The police have you filed as Communists, mind you keep your noses clean.' What's more, our passports had just been stolen. In spite of our prudence we very soon had the police breathing down our necks, so we went to see the officer responsible for arrests concerning crimes of opinion. During our conversation we told him we were convinced that as a policeman he wanted what was good for his country, that he wanted to contribute to the establishment of a healthy and just system of government. We went on to say that he would obtain the opposite result to the one for which he hoped, because by establishing repression the regime inevitably drove young people towards violence and Marxist ideologies. 'I'm a soldier,' he answered, 'my experience is to do with the effectiveness of weapons, that's my business, but I realize that you stand for social justice and honesty and that you are not guilty. I am not expelling you.' We could carry on working freely, and we know that some Christian friends were released after this intervention. Of course dialogue is a risk, but it's the risk of truth.

**GÉRARD.** — In fact I run the risk of having to confess that my passivity is also responsible for the violence the other fellow commits. I'm going to unload all this shameful packet of guilt onto the fellow opposite. We are afraid to confess our fear and, of course, ashamed of our cowardice. I quote from memory this comment from a German pastor: 'When they killed the insane, I said nothing; when they killed the Jews, I said nothing; when they killed the Christians it was too late.'

**HILDEGARD.** — Confessing one's own responsibility

in a conflict is one more step towards truth, and a blow against prejudices. It clears the adversary's path and allows him, with me, to see more clearly the injustice of the situation. To admit one's own weakness, to admit one's share of responsibility, is to allow the truth to act on the conscience of the entry. Its a sort of indirect challenge; the adversary can not help seeing his own responsibility, just as I do mine.

'We must admit that we Christians have not always stood out against violence and injustice. In our weakness and our sin we are sometimes brought to stand witness for exactly the opposite through conniving attitudes towards those who oppress the poor and are at the origins of injustice,' said the Latin-American bishops.[58]

That doesn't mean we have to wallow in our own sinfulness, but rather establish relationships based on truth.

If we put all the evil on the other side and all the good on ours we just set up two monologues on parallel rails. Truth enables us to make crossing-points.

**JEAN.** — This sort of dialogue is not reserved for great world problems. In conjugal conflicts, the little family wars, it works as well, but not automatically, of course. Dialogue in truth is a harsh rock-face; it takes your skin off. I would like to quote an extract from the letter my Catalan friend, Lluis Mario Xirinacs[59] wrote to a member of his country's police force on the 21st March 1976: 'You have beaten me, arrested me, insulted me very often. Do you know what I think, for example, when I am crouching on the ground with my hands on my head, protecting myself from your dreadful truncheon-blows? I feel extremely sad to see you obliged to hit me. It grieves me to be the occasion through which you lose your human dignity by hitting an innocent, defenceless companion. I am ashamed at the accumulation of advantages which have enabled me to choose not to go into the police under this regime, whereas you, because there was no other way out, because you come from a region which is exploited by people from my class, find yourself obliged to play this wretched part. On the one hand, myself, full of possibilities, on the other, you, having fallen into the fateful trap, and reduced to being the hired strongman of the truly privileged. Injustice has made me into a man of studies, and made you into men of violence.'

Truth doesn't come into our mouths just like that, simply because we yawn. It is born of our participation. We must live the truth, says the Gospel. You don't live the truth with ideas, but with your blood, with all your being.

**GÉRARD.** — I have often heard you say that the other person's truth purified your own. When I put myself into the tracks of someone else's truth I give up all that, in my own truth, is petty and personal. In reality each of us cobbles together his own truth in his own way, and then starts barking when another truth appears in his field of vision. The *raison d'être* of scientific publications is to refine truth. Each scientist holds his own version up to the buffeting of the others to see how it stands up to it, and gradually, not without a few scuffles, a discovery is made.

**JEAN.** — There's no need to be timid, to stuff your truth into your pocket and then put your handkerchief on top. You must state clearly and fearlessly what you think is your truth, and show the other fellow in what way his action is unjust. It would be shameful not to condemn a violation of human rights, but this condemnation shouldn't slam the door on a common search for a solution, either.

What do we most often do? We condemn a man, and yet the violations of human beings go on. It's the easy way out. What? There are still people in prison because of their opinions? Still concentration camps? There are still tortures? And yet we have all condemned Hitler, Stalin, Bokassa and Videla, we have condemned all the torturers!

It goes even further. If you come to realize a truth, that truth obliges your conscience. If you betray that truth, that little glimmer of truth, however small it appears in

92

your eyes, you betray your conscience. Don't bother to find out if the pope or the president have made the same discovery as you. You are not responsible before their conscience, but only before your own. Professor Uriel Simon, of Bar-Illan Jewish religious University, founder of the 'Strength and Peace' movement (*Oz Shalom*), launched an appeal supported by two hundred personalities in which he states, among other things: 'The claim to the whole country (including the occupied territories) is bartered for a negation of the individual's basic rights. Religiosity tinged with nationalism is undermining the foundations of law and justice. It is time to fight for a coexistence which rests on a genuine, realistic compromise between Jews and Arabs, and which takes "Israel's" need for security completely into account.'

You mustn't be naive and think that dialogue, at whichever level it takes place, works without difficulties . . . if not worse. In a Nazi concentration camp, a whip was found which had on it the inscription 'Dialogue'.

**HILDEGARD.** — Every man who says a word of truth, even if he is an atheist, lets God speak through him. God is also present in the adversary. This presence will unlock consciences and change attitudes. The most common ways of 'transfiguring', or humanizing the industrial world is through dialogue. The work of our friend Lech Walesa corroborates what I have just said.

**GÉRARD.** — Even so, I feel a little shiver go down my back when I hear you talk like that. All fundamentalists take themselves for God's megaphone. I can still hear them: 'You must listen to me, God is speaking through my mouth, I'm telling you the truth, if you don't believe me' and so on.

**JEAN.** — You can't prevent people from being afraid. They barricade themselves behind God, Marx or Mahomet and shoot anyone who comes within the range of their dogmas.

A word of truth is a word of love and liberty. That means you are prepared to give your life for what you have felt to be true; you will be possessed by it, through thick and thin, but you will never take another person's life or liberty. 'Blockhaus' truths have another characteristic; they are incapable of giving a new face to a situation; Hildegard says 'transfigure'. I don't know any fundamentalist who is not conservative. One imagines non-violent dialogue as if it were a play where we are both author and actor. We arrange everything beforehand, and then, hey presto! the stage villain ends up by being converted by our irrefutable argument.

'Verily, verily, I say unto you, he that believeth in me, the works that I do shall he do also; and greater works than these shall he do, because I go unto my Father (Jn. 14, 12). That's the constructive basis of dialogue; it isn't in my desires, my petty imaginings, it's in my faith. We are astonished by 'unbelievable' solutions discovered by non-violent people, and saddened by those who ape their technique without a drop of inspiration, that is, of Spirit.

GÉRARD. — I had a shock in the Tate Gallery in London when I saw a botched Van Gogh. I was most upset. The following day I went back to the gallery hoping secretly that I had been mistaken. Unfortunately, it was just as bad as before. The visitors in the next room looked shocked when I took my wife Madeleine in my arms and gave her a loud kiss because she had just told me that what I had taken for a Van Gogh was not one; it had been painted by an Englishman. I hadn't looked at the signature because I had recognized Van Gogh's technique. Ah! the technique was perfect.

In the truth capable of piercing our hearts, there is a power which far surpasses those who carry it. With painting as with non-violence it is better not to imitate.

HILDEGARD. — It happened near Olinda, in the north-east of Brazil. A shanty-town had sprung up in a few weeks on private land round a water supply. The owner woke up and set the police machine in motion. Jean and I went there. The word 'poverty' is putting it mildly, but still, the police had their orders to move the people. We had an appointment with the mayor of Olinda; the only technical ability we possessed was the love we had for these brothers and the conviction it was essential to prevent injustice from being done. But the solutions? The mayor found them together with the people. He found funds to buy the land from the absentee owner. The people could obtain the land for a price accessible to them and begin to organize.

**GÉRARD.** — *Dear friend,*
*You know how much (even though I am not at all an expert economist) the essentials of what you have set out link up with what the experience of life has taught me, shared as it has been with those who suffer everywhere, and how much that all links up with the message of the Gospel. Let us help each other together, so that the world may progress along its path willingly, through love, and not only through fear and the blows of misfortune.*[60]

This letter was addressed to Albert Tévoédjré, director of the International Institute of Social Studies, part of the International Labour Organization in Geneva, and it is signed by Abbé Pierre, the founder of the Emmaus communities.

Albert Tévoédjré has published an astonishing book: *The poverty and wealth of the people*, whose preface is by Dom Helder Camara, which is no coincidence. There, we have brought together three men from three different continents, facing the problems of their time.

'What a joy it is to see the people of Africa, Asia and Latin America arrive at the same discoveries, of the greatest importance for their future,' says Dom Helder.

Tévoédjré [61] states that the solution to the violence of despair, frustration and blindness demands a utopia,[62] and I see this in a society of poverty and so of justice; a development based on solidarity, a co-operative republic which encourages better expression of values other than material.

Eliminating homicide and violence is protecting life, the foundation of all solidarity contracts. 'Living is not just existing, it is also having the means of developing one's own participation in the human race.'[63]

**HILDEGARD.** — These three men set up a dialogue reaching across different civilizations in the modern world. None of them takes refuge in a citadel to judge or condemn the world. From the beginning these men came up against an injustice, met men who were despised. They did what their consciences dictated. Today there are Emmaus communities the world over, and the influence of Dom Helder Camara goes well beyond the frontiers of Brazil. New, unexpected solutions spring up when love is the basis of dialogue.

**JEAN.** — Violations of the rights of man in present-day political systems can only create violence. Violence keeps itself going through violence. I think it is a duty to become a 'consciencious objector' when you are faced with this situation. If my conscience doesn't revolt at what is taking place before my eyes, and if it doesn't oblige me to act immediately wherever I can and should act, it's because I'm a liar. That means: 'You see, the Gospel is all very well, excellent, even; but it's made for an ideal world, up in heaven. Meanwhile, well, you've got to live somehow or other, and in life you never achieve your ideal.' Gospel is for saints and naive idiots; 'reality' is for realists and violent people.

**HILDEGARD.** — That's the way we have made very 'rich' theologies and philosophies, which weigh us down to such an extent that we no longer see the essential: man. We anaesthetize our consciences with reassuring political fumes or by practically denying that the Gospel is effective in any way at all. I read recently, in a Catholic periodical[64] that the word 'enemy' when it is used by Christ, can only mean one's personal enemy, and certainly never the public enemy, the one the State decides is my enemy, because in my eyes, he's just a man like any other. You must love your personal enemy, the one who has personally done you harm; as for the other one, the enemy designated by Caesar, you can kill him. You must 'give unto Caesar that which is Caesar's': the corpses of our friends loved by Christ. In German-speaking countries, we say that religion is like women; its place is with the three Ks: *Kirche — Kinder — Küche*, that is, 'in church, with the children and in the kitchen'.

Jesus never taught children; his Word was only for those whose conscience was capable of a response: Yes or No. Being a conscientious objector is the living assertion, in a given historical situation, of a new possibility, an alternative. It would be too easy to limit conscientious objection to those who refuse to do military service. It is a pity that women, who are not concerned by military service do not stand up as 'objectors'; they know better perhaps than men, the value of life; they know it above all in a more concrete way. The women, the mothers who demonstrated on the Plaza de Mayo in Buenos Aires every Thursday, were not practising conscientious objection, they 'were' a living, albeit silent, objection to the terror the government imposed on their country. But be careful! Their objection concerns us, too. Bishop Scharf, of the German Evangelical Church, gave these women the Peace Prize in 1980 and said to his compatriots: 'Listen, look, do not shut your ears or your eyes to the blood spilt on the earth. Denounce crime, so that it may be combated by peaceful action.' German firms and banks supported the Argentine military structures. German and Austrian licences enabled the Argentinian army to build tanks that had no other use than repression. Is it surprising that Argentinia's principal trading partner at that time was the USSR? The problems of armaments and of development are closely linked. They ask each of us the radical question: say 'yes' to armaments and you say 'no' to development in the Third World, that is, to human dignity.

**GÉRARD.** — Saying 'yes' to human dignity leads us straight on to saying 'no' to armaments and even to all armed action. I was an officer, and convinced of the usefulness of military service. One Sunday when I was on duty, my superior, a colonel in the medical corps, was my only table-companion. He was spending his Sunday going through some files on Jehovah's Witnesses; perhaps some of these conscientious objectors could be declared unfit for service on grounds of mental ill-health. There was no law for conscientious objection in France at that time. That suited the commanding officer. I found these young people's attitude absurd. It seemed to me they were giving up, deserting, before the difficulties and the necessities of the real world. 'Putting our stripes aside for a moment,' said the colonel, 'you know, between Christians, Houver, they are right.' I stuck my nose into my plate. A few weeks later I read in the newspaper *Le Monde* that General Paris de Bolardière had resigned from the army in Algeria, to protest against the torture practised by soldiers under the orders of general Massu. De Bollardière said to Massu, who later confirmed it:[65] 'I despise your action.' That was conscientious objection. General de Bollardière was given sixty days prison and then forced to retire early. Since then he has become a non-violent militant. As he no longer knew what to do with his numerous decorations, he sent them to the president. I didn't have General de Bollardière's courage. I continued to believe, like Massu, that you could avoid evil by doing evil. And then, I didn't know the Gosses, but that's no excuse.

**JEAN.** — The Algerian war posed plenty of problems for French non-violent people. We were doing what every non-violent group should do, analysing the conflict. We came to realize that under no circumstances was the war in which our country was engaged justified. From that moment some of us joined the Algerian army fighting against the French army. With some others I went to work in a shanty-town near Paris, where most of the families were Algerian. At first the people who lived there wouldn't have anything to do with us, until the day we replaced a broken window. Ties were made, human ties. Of course we demonstrated to bring home to the whole of France the violence of that war — violence cultivated to the profit of those who were far from Africa, safe and sound behind their bank accounts.

Abbé Pierre was one of the first people in France to propose a special status for conscientious objectors. He was member of Parliament at the time. A colonel, who was a judge on a military court, begged him to take this step. In the name of the law, this military magistrate had sentenced a Jehovah's Witness to prison for the third time in succession, because, in the name of the Gospel, he had refused to learn how to kill, and, in the same session, he had acquitted a German seminarist who, during the retreat through France, had executed some hostages under the threat of his commanding officer's revolver.[66]

My anarchist friend Louis Lecoin fasted at the risk of his life to obtain official recognition for conscientious objectors from the head of state. The president at that time was General Charles de Gaulle. The status of conscientious objector has been caricatured in the law, and even today there are still disputes about it.

An anarchist, a non-believer, risked his life to wring from the State the right for Frenchmen to be free to say 'no' to legalized murder, war and everything that entails. In that 'no' there is already the assertion of man's pre-eminence. Conscientious objection is not just saying 'no' to an adjutant, it is the expression of a new human order.

GÉRARD. — Conscientious objection is a milestone where two powerful institutions — the army and, would you believe it, the churches — met. 'Conscientious objection is too other-worldly, it's utopia, it's defeatism.' Colonel Yves Duval, a good Christian, says: 'You know, I think that Utopia can't get on well with religion . . . or even with any other commitment.'[67] For him, violence is the only recourse when you have to oppose, for example, the butchery of the concentration camps.

The Second Vatican Council did not condemn conscientious objection, but neither did it approve it; it simply asked states to promulgate laws which 'give humane provision for the case of conscientious objectors'.

Through the conflicts they have had with them, dialogue has shown the armed forces that non-violent people are not anti-militarist, which would in itself be a contradiction of terms, if it was not already nonsense from the Christian point of view. But the churches have loads of judgements on the 'objective morality' of the most varied of human situations; there is even a theology for other planets; they all condemn war and are 'indifferent' as far as conscientious objection is concerned.

**JEAN.** — Soldiers have one thing in common with non-violent people: they are ready to give their lives for those they love. They also pay the price, and it has been heavy over this last century! You just have to think of 1914 to 1918, 1939 to 1945, Vietnam and Algeria. The churches flounder about, look for solutions . . . and waste precious time. It took much time and many dead for theologians to begin realizing that a mediaeval war had nothing in common with what happened at Hiroshima!

In 1950, when I asked Monseignor Montini to reconsider the problem of conscientious objectors, he received me standing up, without even asking me to sit down, for twenty minutes. I must say in his defence that I had been unbearable, much more aggressive than now.

'The Church has said all there is to say on this problem', the future Paul VI told me, and I answered: 'Not on your life! For me, non-violence, conscientious objection, is the Gospel, and the Church will never stop discovering the demands of the Gospel.'

I think I know why Paul VI was different to Monseignor Montini: he began to identify himself with those who were suffering, with those who had to bear the rigors of war, he climbed down from his theories, he cried with pain at the United Nations, he cried out the suffering of those killed by war, however 'just' it may be. But he hesitated, he gave a New Year letter on non-violence, adding that one had to 'defend oneself', without specifying how. So you can easily imagine how the Catholic theoreticians and all the others started pushing back the parentheses in order to fit in all the armaments in the world.

Catastrophe! Jesus is in danger! Defend him, prepare the nuclear missiles!

**HILDEGARD.** — The theologians who have abandoned abstract speculations and gone to live among God's people and with him, have become the bearers of the living word of the Gospel. They should, as we also should, become poor, in order to be free before the prophetic word of the assembled people of God. You can read all the articles about conscientious objection, war, defence and armaments; never is the word of Christ or the Gospel pronounced. They only talk about natural law.[68] When will theology become the theology of the people of God?

**JEAN.** — I can answer your question: when the people of God start making theology. We act with regard to theologians in the same way as with soldiers: we let them get on with it; after all, it's their job to defend us and to think for us. Just obey orders and you'll be all right . . .

Discipline, discipline: you'll always be on the right track and you have nothing to worry about. You kill or get killed, but that's of no great importance.

If Jesus Christ isn't 'effective' then we are all idiots, that is, irresponsible. As soon as you get rid of the Gospel you get back to the old pagan 'natural' morality, where you talk about war crimes and governments' right to legitimate defence because, for the moment, 'war has not been eradicated from the human condition, and there is no competent international authority equipped with effective forces, (*Gaudium et Spes*). But it's war that is a crime. Should we Christians have to count on violence to establish peace? And what about the love of the living Christ? What do we do with that? Do we use it before the bombs or after?

**GÉRARD.** — I would like to quote a passage from *Having peace*, by Gaston Bouthoul, the French sociologist who has devoted his life to a study of war and peace. He says: 'The more nations and their leaders sacrifice to the myth of the single state and world government, the more they will feel themselves invested with the sacred mission of founding this state by the sword and by fire. Nowadays, the great political ideas lead all too often to this appealing programme: we will start by destroying a generation, and then we will see about universal happiness.'[69] All our political leaders, whatever their party, want our happiness, and they are all prepared, if necessary, to start a nuclear war in order to make our happiness even greater.

'Workers of the world, kill each other', say the Communists: while others say: 'Cut each other's throats in order to defend the supreme values of man'.

I'm ashamed of indulging in macabre humour. Faced with the madness in which I live there are not many ways out.

**HILDEGARD.** — All situations of injustice and violence, and that is what war is all about, are like spinning tops; if nobody gives the energy needed to make them turn and stand upright, they fall over. It is very important to draw up an inventory of all the sources of energy which keep a situation of violence going. We can not allow ourselves not to analyse these forces very clearly, for they can also change and become the driving force of justice and peace.

In Sao Paulo, in Brazil, the nine hundred workers at a cement works went on strike for seven years in order to be treated as humans. They realized that the Church was one of the forces which kept up the unjust system that reduced them to poverty. In spite of everything, they had enough faith in man to get in touch with these bishops who lived so far from them. By their testimony they persuaded thirty-five bishops to sign a petition to the president in their favour. From that moment, the Cardinal of Sao Paulo was actively on the side of the workers. These workers had another very powerful force against them; the media. For the journalists things were very simple: strikers equal Communists. With their lawyer, Mario de Jésus, the workers tackled the press. The truth about the movement was eventually published in the largest Sao Paulo daily, *O Estado de Sao Paulo*. From that moment there was a change in public opinion.

Conscientious objectors and non-violent people can get the world out of the infernal spiral of modern warlike violence by telling the truth about forces that keep it alive. All situations of violence have the same source: lies. War is no exception.

And if nowadays in almost all countries, politics reminds us of a cynical play, that's because we are beginning to see the lies through the gaps in the scenery.

I am just quoting a few examples: in 1980 *Le Monde* announced that West Germany was delivering to the Soviet Union a factory for producing artillery shells; in February 1981 Paris and Tripoli were almost at war over Chad, and yet Libyan pilots were training on Super-Frelon helicopters (70 million francs each) in Marseilles.[70]

**GÉRARD.** — Not many trains pass through my village any more, so you can walk along the railway, and that's where I made an interesting discovery. On one rail I read *De Wendel Hayange* in French, and on the other, in German, *Von Wendel, Hayingen*. Wars are always won by the same people!

Jean-Jacques Servan-Schreiber stated recently what historians have suspected for a long time: 'The attack on Pearl Harbour surprised no-one except those who died there, certainly not Roosevelt, who knew the date and the time.'[71]

I could go on and on giving examples, but you can't remake history. What can we, the ordinary people, the nameless ones, the 'other ranks' do about it? It's like an ant taking on an elephant . . .

**JEAN.** — Jesus says it very clearly: 'Without me you

can do nothing' (Jn. 15,5). To put it another way, if we cut ourselves off from that source of love which is Jesus, truth, justice, love, everything we do will dry up like rotten wood. The only force that can unify man is love; everything else cuts him into bits, and plants division in him, and incites war. Try it. As soon as you start dealing in morality you put yourself on the side of Good. You are one of the Goodies, and on the other side you have all the rest, the Others. As soon as you love, you love the other one for what he is, because you are permeable to love, it flows from you to the others. Once you are connected to the source the rest will be added unto you. The rest begins with commitment. Love is not a cloud wandering high up in the sky. It's hands, faces, hearts; it's Life there where you are, immediately.

I am often told: 'You know, Jean, we're going to seek God, we're going to get ready, and then we'll get down to work.' Two years later they are still getting ready, and still fishing for God. You've got to find out what is going on, but information is not constructing theories, it's an element of the action which becomes part of our education as the action develops. People say: 'Yes, but with your system we run the risk of making mistakes which could be quite serious.' That's true, I accept errors, they are part of the process, and they enable us to make adjustments. The Americans had planned for all eventualities when they went to the moon, all the circuits had been tripled, but they still had failures. So what? Did that prevent them going to the moon?

You mustn't cheat yourself or other people. If you have love within you as small as a grain of mustard seed, you can do everything, as long as you don't crush it.

I don't understand: Christians have the Spirit of love, and they think that it's up to them to plan everything, do everything by themselves, because, no doubt, otherwise it would not be done properly.

GÉRARD. — Why don't you say what has to be done?

**JEAN.** — Ah! That's too much! The police, governments, the priests and the bosses all tell you what you should do. All these 'authorities' are only interested in you in order to tell you what you should do: you should be obedient, you should be a number who pays, who kills and is killed when ordered to. But you are so used to being another that you are completely lost when you are asked to be yourself and to act by yourself.

Non-violence by numbers doesn't work. It doesn't work all by yourself, either. You aren't non-violent single-handed, any more than you can be a Christian shut up in your little tower.

**HILDEGARD.** — Non-violent action is fundamentally creative. It makes each particular individual discover the latent forces of truth within himself and put them into action with imagination and initiative. Non-violence is a liberating force, quite the contrary to the forces and principles which govern our consumer society, which aim to control and dominate men's desires and actions.

The true solutions to the conflicts and problems non-violent people have to face can only be found in communal action carried out by a basic group. In such a group, the creative contribution of each one is acknowledged and indispensible.

In the basic group someone can have a particular part to play, for example, organizing, but he is not the leader, that is, someone who decides for the others. In the group, each person finds the place which corresponds to his capacities, to his personal charisma in respect for the others. At the intersection of all the diverse personalities of which the group is made up, you will find, in general, a member who tries to unite through love without ever trying to impose uniformity.

A non-violent group excludes nobody; it can embrace young and old, sick and healthy, people of widely differing cultural levels. It's a characteristic of non-violent groups and non-violent struggles: everyone can take part, since every man and every woman is acknowledged as such and not catalogued according to their age, sex, fortune, cultural level and religious denomination. The group works out the action, and each one takes it upon himself to keep steadfastly to the decisions taken in common.

**JEAN.** — The peasants of the Larzac in the southwest of France have proved the effectiveness of a non-violent community in relation to the military administration and the French state. Whole families have taken part in the struggle — even sheep have their part to play.

In 1971, the mayor of Saint-Jean-de-Bruel, a little village on the Larzac plateau, in the Aveyron department, set up a defence committee for the Larzac because the government had decided to enlarge the military camp which was in the region. With this project, the area of the camp would go from 3,000 hectares to 17,000 hectares, and it would kick sheep farmers off their land. The *préfet* promised to negotiate with the farmers, but the government transferred him and decided to go ahead with the extension. In spite of being officially banned, 6,000 people demonstrated their opposition to the project at Millau. The next day, the Bishop of Rodez and the priests of the Millau area came out in favour of the farmers. On the 6th December 1971, the Aveyron Council asked the Minister of Defence to postpone the project. The Minister's answer was: 'The extension will be made'. In February the farmers went into action: they lit large fires on the hills and rang the church bells, which put the police into turmoil. At the same time they distributed leaflets in Millau. And then, my friends Lanza del Vasto and Jean Toulat arrived, both of them non-violent people. Lanza fasted for two weeks; with him a hundred-and-three farmers signed a pact by which they undertook to stay on the Larzac whatever happened. The fast had cemented their unity. On the 16th October, five Larzac farmers took sixty sheep to Paris, to graze under the Eiffel Tower. All the press was there. At last the whole of France was beginning to hear about the Larzac.

The government, however, did not yield an inch. On

the contrary! On the 7th January 1973, the 'Larzacs' set out for Paris on their tractors. Their success with the ordinary people was so great that the police stopped them at Orleans. But that didn't matter! They continued on foot, and their fellow farmers in the region let them use their tractors.

'When we arrived in Paris we had achieved our goal. We wanted to sensitize public opinion, and we had succeeded. We had shown our problem in public, and we had also learnt about the problems of others. Through these struggles, united and standing together, we will oblige those who exploit us and oppress us to think again.'[72]

In April 1975, fifty farmers sent their military papers back to the Ministry of Defence: that was civil disobedience. On the 25th and the 26th of August 1973, 30,000 people demonstrated their solidarity with the Larzac farmers and with their struggle. On the 16th and 17th of August, 103,000 people came to celebrate the harvest on the plateau. It was the first harvest for the Third World; instead of arms the 'Larzacs' sent wheat. Wheat creates life.

**HILDEGARD.** — It is now 1981; the farmers have come back to Paris, the struggle is going on and life is still in the hands of a few sheep-farmers.

The imagination of these men and women has literally recreated non-violent tactics. They have found ways of action which are worth thousands of speeches, and the way their struggle is rooted in truth and an unshakeable love of life has attracted the support and sympathy of many people throughout France and the whole world.

The effectiveness and the strength of direct actions is conditioned by how much truth penetrates through them and deeply affects people who were, at first, indifferent. It is essential that those who embark on a direct action persevere in their non-violent attitude, whatever happens. There has been no shortage of provocations on the Larzac, yet the farmers have never fallen into the trap of violence.

107

## ANNEXE II

On the 3rd June 1981, President François Mitterand announced the cancellation of the project to extend the camp.

*The Larzac, 4th June, 1981*

M. Jean Goss,
Vienna, Austria.

*Dear friend,*

*We needed to be guided, and you were among us. The teaching we received has shown us forever how strong and rich non-violence is.*

*Today we are overwhelmed by an immense happiness.*

*Witnesses of this long struggle, we will continue in faith the work already begun.*

*Christiane*
*For the Larzac farmers*

# VII

GÉRARD. — If I understand correctly, direct action is inspired by a basic core around which other people and other movements gather, in order to be more effective in their struggle. Now the same thing happens for non-violence as happens for churches: there are dozens of different factions, and none of them can get on with the others! Jesus' disciples didn't give us a good example of teamwork . . .

JEAN. — It's true, we haven't yet got used to working freely together. We work together out of necessity, not out of love. We hang on to our differences, and each of us is afraid of losing our identity in communal work. As if life resided in those things that differentiate us from each other! 'He who loses his life will save it; he who saves his life will lose it.' Life is unique, but its form is multiple. Perhaps one day, Christians will have no more ecumenical problems once they start making fire with a couple of flints again.

We Christians possess a wealth of different theologies, liturgies and traditions, whereas our only wealth should be Jesus Christ.

HILDEGARD. — I have suffered a lot, and I don't think I am the only one, from the absence of a community of faith. It exists officially, of course; there are churches and there are the clergy. Yet real communities are born; I have met them above all in Latin America. There there is no romantic halo around the word community. It's a vital necessity.

Here in Europe, we haven't got that far yet. We are not

used to basing our relations on trust, to listening to the word of God together and answering it with a concrete commitment. But there are new non-violent communities developing in many parts of Europe. They are a sign of hope.

**JEAN.** — Have you ever walked in the snow behind a friend? At first you try to walk in his steps to save energy, to do the same as he does. You inevitably fall flat on your face, or at least you feel something's wrong. Well, that's exactly what happens in non-violence. Each one must make his own tracks: Gandhi, King and Dolci don't make tracks, they show the direction, the orientation.

Jesus doesn't walk for you, he says that clearly: 'I am the way'. The first Christians lived in community, that's very good, but it doesn't mean that if we all live together under the same roof we'll be like the first Christians. If you want love to circulate between men you will have to invent new forms of non-violence.

**GÉRARD.** — Non-violent action is only possible with men and women who have a backbone, people who exist in their own right, who are not held up by the crutches of 'general esteem' and 'respect', but who are sufficiently down to earth to be aware of their limits, so that they listen when other people speak to them. With such a crowd you don't make an army where discipline is the driving force.

**JEAN.** — When it comes down to it, non-violent action has just one watchword: 'liberty'. Civil disobedience, the refusal to obey an unjust law, to support an unjust government, is a way of preventing men from being slaves to other men.

The most typical example is Gandhi's salt march in March 1930. The British, very cleverly, had imposed a monopoly of 'their' salt on India, and filled the holds of their ships with it. They killed at least two birds with one stone, because, in fact, they made themselves the masters

110

of all the Indian farmers, whose cattle needed salt as much as the farmers themselves. After a march of 200 miles, Gandhi and his friends arrived at a little village beside the sea, and there, symbolically, the Mahatma picked up a few grains of salt, fresh salt. He encouraged people to make fresh salt, to make salt a symbol of freedom. The British didn't just let them get on with it. They filled up the prisons. Gandhi was there on the 4th May, but the result was very different from what the British had expected; they didn't sell anything any more. Now 'where your treasure is, there your heart is also'; their pockets had bled too much, so they got Gandhi out of prison and started negotiating.

Men who have great inner liberty, who are capable of taking on acts of civil disobedience with all their consequences (you must always see the action and the consequences at the same time) are difficult people to get on with. Without that solid core of inner freedom, non-violence is not effective, but that also explains the pig-headedness of some non-violent people. You can understand that people who like order, regulations and the law, hide their faces in front of fellow citizens who are difficult to label.


**HILDEGARD.** — Martin Luther King had felt what Jean is talking about, and was greatly saddened by it. In a letter written in Birmingham prison, he said, 'The superficial understanding of well-wishers is more disappointing than the total incomprehension of adversaries. Luke-warm acceptance is more off-putting than out-and-out refusal.'[73] Men prefer order to justice. That maxim props up all the world's dictatorships. They all have the same slogan, the same 'ideal', *order*, and at the Nuremberg trials, the Nazis had only carried out 'orders'. But even that is only a façade. We don't prefer order to justice; we are afraid of freedom. Churches, political parties and ordinary people are afraid of non-violence because they are afraid of freedom, and their own freedom above all. But that is the same for all confessions.

111

**GÉRARD.** — It's true, it's more convenient to receive your freedom from someone else's hands than to go and get it in the depths of your own heart, because that can be a very painful experience.

'We are free to accept or reject becoming free, that is where autonomy lies, much more than in actions, which are only the results. This is the crucial act for the individual, and through him, for society.'[74]

That, no doubt, is why Gandhi said: 'Civil disobedience demands a much greater preliminary preparation, and much more self-control than non co-operation.'[75]

**HILDEGARD.** — There is a difference between non co-operation and civil disobedience. If you refuse to buy veal fed on hormones you refuse to co-operate with a system in which profit is put before health, and so before human dignity. It is a very effective non-violent action, but it is a long way from demanding of those who apply it an inner determination similar to that demanded by a collective decision to send back one's military papers. That is at least true for this particular example.

In non co-operation, as in civil disobedience, the action is not that of an isolated individual; it's a communal action, whose preparation should also be communal.

By that I do not mean that individual actions are worthless. No, but I just want to say that the chances of being effective are much greater with mass action.

**GÉRARD.** — In the list of books on non-violence, the large majority analyse non-violent techniques and non-violent strategies.

We only have to listen to you two to realize that all that is not enough. You say, 'On every occasion you must hold onto the non-violent character of the dialogue, the demonstration or the civil disobedience that is to respect the adversary in each non-violent action.'

But there is more to it than that. There is a sort of osmosis between military language and non-violent language. Everyone talks about weapons; on the one hand, bombs, on the other, heavy non-violent weapons. Both sides talk about strategy, battles and so on. What worries me is that non-violence loses its identity in all that. We make war, but we live on love. If we go on trying to find correspondences whose aim, above all, is immediate effectiveness, the time will come when the difference between the two strategies will be just a practical one. 'I'm too weak to hit you, but I've found a clever way of getting my own back.' Am I exaggerating? We all have such an impression that we exist more when we can diminish someone else. 'If you are the king of the Jews, save yourself!' (Luke 23. 37).

JEAN. — Do you know why soldiers the world over march in step and do arms drill?

GÉRARD. — Explain.

JEAN. — You can't 'shoulder arms' or 'quick march' and think about what you are doing at the same time, and have your brain in normal working order. It's impossible. You miss a step, you use the wrong shoulder. It's the same principle as working on a production line. You end up with a man for whom it is no longer possible to be, who is morally headless.

Non-violence insists that each of us become a human being. There are recipes for killing a man morally, but there are none for helping him to be born. You can be taught what you must do if you want to paint, but not how to make a picture. That's something you must do all by yourself. I think you can give people the basic essentials of non-violence, but you're making a big mistake if you think you just have to take a correspondence course to become non-violent.

The first condition of non-violence is that you must 'be'. I am Jean. I'm not the gentleman who gives lectures, the trade unionist, railwayman, the fellow who was once decorated by the French army, the non-violent rabble-rouser. No. I am Jean. If I slip into the costume of one of these characters, even if it is the non-violent prophet of the Almighty, then I am no longer Jean; I am in the cinema, and non-violence doesn't go along with the cinema. Jean is fond of good food, Jean is violent, Jean has loads of weaknesses . . . right, O.K., I am Jean. God loves Jean as Jean is, so I don't see why Jean should go and make a mask to hide his weaknesses.

Why is it so easy for us to be violent? Because we are afraid we will die if one of these masks is torn off.

The states, the powerful of this world, have so much influence on us because they manipulate these little for-external-use-only beings of ours.

As long as we don't realize what we are, we live in unconsciousness, and there nothing touches us; we sleep.

On the other hand, there is a fashion, a race even, to personal realization. Everyone wants enlightenment, awakening, *samadhi, satori*, realization and liberation. What for?

You can stand on your head or stay on your knees for ten years. You will still, one day, have to 'kiss the leper' if you want to be free.

'Clean', 'hygienic' liberation, without getting your hands dirty or without chafing your shoulders with the wood of someone else's cross, is an illusion. It's *maya*.

**HILDEGARD.** — Until 1976, the peasants of Alagamar, in Brazil, didn't even know they were persons. For their 'owners', they were a breed for slaves who worked the land. For the bishop of that region, they were so many souls! The owner wanted to kick the peasants off the land so as to make more money. Injustice woke them up; they found themselves to be human beings and persons standing up for themselves. They gathered together; they even built a chapel. The owner ordered his private police to demolish this place of 'subversion' where the peasants 'intoxicated' themselves with the Gospel. The Archbishop, José Maria Pires, came, and discovered men struggling for justice. What's more, when he went back to his cathedral, he said from the pulpit: 'These peasants whom we despise, whom we disdain, are really living the Gospel'. Every time a man really exists, he provokes other people in their existence, but also in their liberty. They can react through good as through evil. We come back to the law of all or nothing 'He who is not for me is against me.' This spark that starts it all off — 'you don't know where it comes from or where it goes.'

**GÉRARD.** — But once this inner revolution has begun, how does it continue? Don't you need a guide from time to time to point out where you are going wrong, and emphasize the essential?

**HILDEGARD.** — The yogis have a proverb that says: 'When the disciple is ready the master arrives.' I realize that putting it like that, it could look as if I am evading the question, but neither Jean nor I have ever seen a friend 'touched' by non-violence who has not found his path, on one condition, which is obvious. That is that he should be committed, that is to say that in one way or another his being should take on 'body', and that what has happened within him become visible to everyone. The forms of commitment are as varied as the men who take them, and no-one can impose a commitment on someone else from the outside.

**JEAN.** — Very often during our tours, people who listen to us are astonished to see that we can't pull solutions out of a hat for problems ranging from non-violent education of young children to nuclear war. That's the system: 'Vote for me and I'll think for you, so you can sleep peacefully.' Is that right?

Non-violence urges man towards his own freedom; that's the path, there is no other. Doctrines, even if they call themselves non-violent, are justifications of freedom, and 'justification is born of freedom in order to destroy it'.[76] When men start justifying freedom they sometimes end up killing in its name.

115

In our brains, there is still the couplet 'revolution-liberty' which could also be expressed 'violence-liberty'.

'You see,' I am told, 'the French Revolution brought liberty; the Russian Revolution brought liberty,' etc. That's true, but the revolution brought liberty *in spite* of violence, and not because of it. Violence is a reactionary weapon and not revolutionary. You just have to look around you to realize what methods all dictatorships throughout the world and throughout history use: lies, torture, political murder, hatred, injustice, exploitation of men and domination, open or latent. One word sums all that up: violence. Now what are the bases of all great revolutions? Truth, justice, solidarity, human rights, respect for men, love. It's easy to sum up: *non-violence*. The bases of revolutions are their means and their goal at one and the same time. What all true revolutionaries want, and what, when it comes down to it, all men desire, is a society where violence is replaced by liberty and respect for everyone. Violence puts brakes on revolution, what is worse, aborts it; the Soviet example is obvious, and Franco's Spain confirms it even more. Liberty is frightening, I know, and yet it is the risk of God.

**HILDEGARD.** — Since the 6th August 1945, man's liberty has changed. Whether we like it or not, each of us has become responsible for humanity. He or she is not only responsible for him or herself, but also for mankind. These are not just words. 'We are driven back to our liberty through our own liberty.' The choice is not between one weapon and another, but between life and death. This is no desperate choice; love, life, are always as powerful as their enemy, even in our time. We are all, whether we realize it or not, faced with this choice which men have never before had to make.

I don't know if history is an eternal repetition, but I know that, historically, a situation like this has not previously existed on this planet.

**GÉRARD.** — It's enough to make you panic. I realize

the phenomenal danger that hangs over us. I'm not the only one, and at the same time I realize how powerless I am in relation to this monster that is getting ready to devour all men. I'm completely overwhelmed. What good is it if I scream in the privacy of my own room?

**JEAN.** — None at all, apart from frightening yourself or the neighbour's cat. Dom Helder Camara has said: 'When we dream alone it is only a dream. When we dream together, it's the beginning of reality.'[77]

But we must go beyond this stage. We must dream out loud and in all languages. We still think we must defend ourselves, we the little Jean Goss, the little Gérard Houver. No, all men are in danger, not only the French, the Russians and the Americans. The non-violent struggle begins in each one of us, but must be carried on at all levels, regional, national and international.

My friend Rachel Goettmann says that if Christians lived the Gospel there would be no need for non-violent movements. Non-violence would be as vast as the world. The love of Christ begins in our hearts. His transforming action through the Spirit fills the world . . . if we give him our voice. The tacit acceptance of violence by all Christian denominations is a poison which infiltrates and paralyses the fabric of the Church. The churches find themselves bound to the dominating and murderous violence of the states. This poison gags the truth of the Gospel and prevents it from being a word of active liberation capable of saving all men, by shutting it up in religious particularism.

Nowadays, the Gospel is still imprisoned in temples, but it is made for public places. Can you imagine what our world would be like if Saint Francis or Saint Vincent de Paul had just bothered about their own little personal conversion?

**HILDEGARD.** — Since Hiroshima we have known the true face of violence: total murder. That can also make us discover the true face of truth, of the love of Christ. When

117

I say 'discover', I mean 'remove the rags and finery we have dressed it up in'; then truth acts because it is truth.

'If you love me, keep my commandments, and I will pray the father, and he shall give you another comforter, that he may abide with you for ever; even the spirit of truth, whom the world cannot receive, because it seeth him not, neither knoweth him: but ye know him, for he dwelleth with you, and shall be in *you*' (John 14. 15–17).

The reality of this love, the experience we can have of this truth, this liberty within ourselves, is the only force we can set against violence.

Girard says, 'Faced with the nuclear threat there is only the pertinence of the text of the Gospel. I say this: the words are there, these words provoke us and beseige us. These words call out to us as individuals, these words crush us all. I think that by revealing their own power they accuse all churches and all atheisms.'[78]

**GÉRARD.** — 'He who seeks emptiness finds emptiness. He who seeks or desires something, seeks and desires emptiness. But to him who seeks and desires nothing but God alone, God "uncovers" and gives everything he has hidden in his divine heart, so that he may possess it completely, like God.' I quote a sermon by Meister Eckhart[79] because it illustrates what you have just said, and gives meaning to the preparation of non-violent action as it does to commitment. As long as we are afraid of the contradictions which can slip into our commitment, we live at their level and are not very effective. We must let love shine through these contradictions in order to unite them on another level.

**JEAN.** — That's true. There is no completely non-violent trade union, no non-violent political party, not even a non-violent church. Whatever I do, alas, will always be shaky. What is evangelical is not the perfection of institutions, but the love we bring to them. It doesn't matter what the sign on the outside says if inside there is

118

someone to feed the hungry, clothe the naked and release those who are prisoners.

Fifty million human beings, among whom were thirteen million children, starved to death in 1980. We are coming to a historical moment, when we have no longer any choice. Nowadays we must, above all, take what God has revealed to us through Jesus Christ, what God has offered us through his only son: his Love, his Way, his Law of Truth and Love! Either we will live that, and the world will be saved, or we will refuse it and the world will be lost. But I'm sure we are going to take it, and live it. Many among the poor have already chosen. We, who are rich in everything, we the intellectuals, we are those who must be converted, we must proclaim his active, aggressive, creative and redeeming love which will save us all, for He is the Way, the Truth and the Life.

**GÉRARD.** — Intellectuals are proclaiming God as never before. He has become a best-seller. Christians take up commitments in all sectors of our society, but these commitments are often diametrically opposed to each other. There are military Christians and conscientious objectors, there are Christians in the left-wing parties and in the conservative parties. The ecclesiastical authorities in all churches are divided in the same way: for the bomb or against it. What a mess it all is! Wouldn't it be easier to leave all those people standing there, who go on and on thinking up clever, subtle ideas while the universe goes to rack and ruin, and go and see those who are not bogged down with doctrinal preoccupations from another age in order to carry out effective non-violent action? The Gospel, for individuals, is fine, excellent even, but it makes a barrier between you and those who have nothing to do with it and, in the end, prevents non-violence from being accessible to everyone.

**JEAN.** — You don't want me to cut my head off in order to be a success, do you? Because that's exactly what you have just told me to do. You mustn't confuse a barrier

119

with a stumbling block. The Lord does not set up a barrier between myself and the others. If there is a barrier, it's me. When you stub your toe on a stone on the path, because you hadn't seen it, you begin to realize you were living on the moon, and you start paying attention to where you put your feet again. A stumbling-block is exactly that. That's what the Gospel is — a return to reality. I don't manufacture a pre-programmed non-violence, a sort of scientific theory. I stumble against the beatitudes.

Of course I don't parade God around, but if I didn't speak the Word that makes life, if I strangled the source that makes me love, it would be suicide, lying to myself and to others. It is as if I were to take off my wedding-ring to pretend I was single. But because I bear witness to the love that has been granted me, and which has given me no rest for more than forty years, that doesn't mean I have either the pretention or the desire to convert someone.

Truth doesn't belong to Jean Goss. My job is to present it, offer it and say it with my poverty and my strength.

**GÉRARD.** — In 1972, I was witness to a very important decision in your life. You left the International Fellowship of Reconciliation (IFOR), of which you were secretaries, and which you yourselves had spread over the continents. The reason for this resignation was that the Fellowship, on the international level, had renounced its evangelical basis. I saw your doubts and I saw how you gave yourselves up to the Lord; you chose the exodus, evangelical nomadism . . . Which is still going on.[80]

**HILDEGARD.** — Giving up the struggle for the total liberation of man is denying one's faith in Jesus the liberator. There is no separation between faith and life, between faith and the revolutionary transformation of unjust society. That is an answer to your question, because some could think that faith is a handicap in non-violent liberation; they see faith as something else, on another

120

level, higher up and further off, and it has nothing to do with these day-to-day social or political struggles, because it would risk being polluted. For some, faith embraces active non-violence, and for others, non-violence makes faith impure. That partly explains the mistrust of the churches with regard to evangelical non-violence, even if certain bishops have become martyrs because of it, as is the case with our friend Monseignor Romero in El Salvador. To live and act through the strength of non-violence is to discover and allow to act, in man, the force that the Father revealed to us in Jesus Christ. he made himself humble, he became part of this earth, he was made of our clay. To our revolt, our hatred and our injustices, he has only had one answer: his love. But is that so hard to see? Are we blind? Evil and injustice can only be overcome by the strength of justice and love. Love for one's enemies and love for God.

**JEAN.** — We have tried everything; popes have made just wars and Christians have made 'Christian' political parties. The socialists came along; they thought evil came from the alienation of man by religion and by other men. They made wars, even wars between socialist countries. And what about Stalin? Do you really want me to be quiet, and not say the truth about Jesus? Every time we use violence we are prisoners of violence; there is no break in the chain. Every time we live on love we break a link in the chain of violence.

Are those who say they believe in love going to incarnate it? I don't know. I don't give an answer, I give all my strength, all my time, all my life. That passage from Saint John (9.1–3) often comes to my mind where the disciples ask Jesus a question about a man born blind: 'Who did sin, this man or his parents, that he was born blind?' and Jesus answered, neither hath this man sinned, nor his parents: but that the works of God should be made manifest in him.'

The blind man is our world, with its suffering, its sin and its hunger, and it's up to us to make the manifestation of God flow into it. To do that there is only Christ's method. All the others have demonstrated that they only increase the blindness.

**GÉRARD.** — Don't you think it could be possible to found a non-violent political party, or a large non-violent movement?

**HILDEGARD.** — We find ourselves in a world without precedent; our situation has not been experienced by men before. We only know the cause of the tragedy, and not its future development.

We know that violence is the mother of planetary fear. We try to apply 'recipes' to this situation which have been used in situations we think are analogous. But doubtless no one has ever lived through what we are living through at the end of the twentieth century. We are obliged to innovate, and to innovate radically. All going back to the past seems to be forbidden. Every time we have recourse to violence, however slight it is, it is a step towards the abyss of total violence. Little wars only prepare the way for the big one, just as our little violences fatten the planet's violence.

The non-violent movement is the property of no one, of no party and no group. Through this question you put your finger on the essence of our vocation as a couple. We didn't choose our 'international' life, it was thrust upon us. Jean doesn't spend even a month in his country of origin, France. We are very often separated from each other. While Jean is in Belgium, Lebanon or Poland, the Lord calls me to south Africa, Salvador or Britain.

We don't try to create a sort of 'supranational non-violence party'. At each meeting, we speak of God's unshakeable confidence in man, in which reside the strength and the capacity for transformation, the insistence on liberty. We refuse no one; Christ spoke to everyone. The choice of non-violence demands the participation of everyone. The scientists in our modern industrial societies are responsible for our environment, the armed forces owe us the truth about armaments and their consequences, but they are also responsible for a non-violent civil defence. Non-violent commitment should be taken up by medical doctors and biologists. Wherever the major problems of our time are decided on, wherever there is an inevitable choice between degradation and absolute respect for human life, the presence of non-violent people is necessary.

The Christian, the disciple of Jesus, the non-violent liberator, is not only challenged by the crisis humanity is facing, he or she should also be committed to it as a witness of non-violent liberation.

**JEAN.** — From the political point of view I should mention two movements I feel particularly concerned with. I cite them without wishing to belittle the others; I am speaking of what I know best, that is, what is nearest my heart. In 1974, the M.A.N. (Movement for a Non-violent Alternative) was created: it is composed of about thirty non-violent groups, including the Orleans Non-violent Community. Jean-Marie Muller is a founder-member of the M.A.N. 'If we join together in one movement, it is, on the one hand, so that we ourselves may have a deeper understanding of the specific contribution non-violence has to make to the struggle for justice and liberty, and, on the other hand, to engage in a dialogue with our political partners, in order to explore together what non-violence can contribute to present-day debates and combats. Therefore the goal of M.A.N. is not in itself; it sets out to be a means of struggle, an instrument that enables the specific contribution of non-violence to be put to good use and to prevail.'[81]

The second experience is totally different. A group threw itself into direct political action: election campaigns, local and regional responsibilities. One of its members became mayor of a small town of 7,000 inhabitants, and then regional councillor. I didn't believe it, and I was astounded when, by chance, I was able to follow part of his election campaign. Will he carry on? Will others follow his example? I don't know. One thing I am sure of is that the grace of God has breathed upon him, that he has accepted it and tried to incarnate it. Every one of us should do that, wherever the Lord has put him, in his particular situation, his profession, his school, his political party and so on. That's when non-violence becomes possible. Love is only possible in a heart that is beating.

**GÉRARD.** — Will he carry on? Will others follow his example? I had to get this clear, so I quite simply went and asked the person concerned: 'Joseph, since 1973 you have been involved in politics in the spirit of non-violence. Have you never reconciled this activity in the service of the town and the region with belonging to a political party?' He answered, 'Parties are like sects: I've got my truth, there is only my truth. I can't join up with a battalion of defenders of this truth, it's against my nature. I am at the service of citizens, not at the service of an authority or of power. The "Christian" label on certain parties is just electoral publicity. Christians working in political parties have a hard life. The party's need to be effective often crushes evangelical truth. I know that in politics everything, really everything can be justified, but there are some things I just can't swallow. It is possible to be a Christian in a political party provided you tell the truth and do not condone dishonesty. Under those conditions you don't stay very long in these political centres. That doesn't mean I lead an easy life; I realize that man is made to love, and loving means giving. It's very easy to say that in front of you, but when, in the name of this law, I must say "no" to someone who wants to swindle the community, who wants to dominate and take advantage of others, I am less sure of myself. He is also a man loved by Christ, and whom I should love.'

I asked him if he could refer to a model. He said, 'No I can't; all models of non-violence are men of crisis, and I am concerned with humdrum day-to-day affairs; there are no major crises in my little part of the country. I must manage everyday problems in the spirit of non-violence, put myself into the hands of the Gospel every day. Human beings need someone to give himself for them. I think I have not been asked to make the same gift as Monseignor Romero. I am asked to deal with more down-to-earth things, such as old people's associations, tourism and roads. You must recreate the model every morning, and, above all, realize that you don't resemble it. Other people only rarely understand.'

I asked him if he thought it would last. He responded, 'I am not a fortune-teller. I know the conditions that will allow it to last. Neither myself nor my friends have the right to attach non-violence to our own persons. This "kind of politics" can only last in people's hearts; it can not be shut up in a group. This kind of politics can only last if it gets across to young people through witness, dialogue and the Spirit. Non-violence in action only inspires because it is linked to those who are prophets in the world. Prophets, who must not be confused with ministers, whether they are of religion or of politics, are men who "take part" in our world and in the world of the Gospel.'

Jean, a man, who was your friend went to join his Lord not very long ago. The last time you were seen together was at Saint-Séverin in 1978 when you were fasting with other non-violent people in union with the Larzac farmers and Lanza del Vasto, the non-violent patriarch.

**JEAN.** — Lanza, disciple of Gandhi, founder of the Arche community, poet, writer, musician, scholar and non-violent. He fasted during the Vatican Council, during the Algerian war and in the Larzac. He opposed the proliferation of nuclear power stations. We were different, and believe me, with our characters we sometimes had to use all the riches of non-violent strategy in order to get on with each other. With him, non-violence had literally taken root, had become one with the earth. 'With us, he who cultivates the soil cultivates himself at the same time. After all, the man of the soil is a complete man.'[82] Non-violence has no stereotype. I have only lived a short time

125

in the country, and sometimes I like to think it would be nice to be ill and be mollycoddled a little bit. Travelling often disturbs our family life, it's the opposite of the well-ordered life of a rural community. And yet . . . for Lanza as for me, non-violence is an absolute. 'If it is not an absolute it doesn't resist attacks,'[83] says Lanza.

On my journeys I find myself among men and women for whom religious problems have little, or even no importance. With them just as with those who live by faith, my work always begins by involvement in a non-violent 'action' against our injustice.

The grace of God is the strength he gives you to respect man while at the same time you see injustice growing around you, and to respect man absolutely. Man is the absolute. Look at yourself in the mirror and tell me if what you see is concrete. God is in every man, so he's going to help you respect the other fellow, the one who does you wrong.

**HILDEGARD.** — Non-violent behaviour is possible for every man. Since this attitude is not abstract but living, it must be reconquered every day in order to develop. It is like life — a struggle. There will never be any disarmament if it stays on the level of diplomatic abstractions. The 'authorities' talk about it only to end up saying that it is not possible, even if it was desirable. Disarmament is a struggle. In this struggle truth is by far the most important thing. We must tell the truth about armaments, about the effectiveness of arms in conflicts, for protection and for profit.

It is not as simple as that; the arms merchants are the warmongers, but how can we conceive Socialist, or Communist arms merchants?

For Sean MacBride, the founder of Amnesty International and Nobel Peace Prize winner 'The struggle for peace and disarmament is the most important, as crucial as the one for human rights in the 60s,'[84] and in his eyes the major obstacle to disarmament is 'the refusal of the military class to accept this generalized disarmament.'[85]

There is obviously an 'arms international' which goes beyond political ideologies.

**JEAN.** — When you simplify problems you fall into the trap of the 'you only have to' philosophy! Disarmament is no simpler than any other human problem, and I don't intend to resolve it by magic. I would like to ask some questions to show how we can find the levers that enable us to change an established situation:

'Who are arms made by?' By workers who, here in the West, at least, are unionized.

'Who are arms handled by?' By soldiers who, in the West, speak and tell their truth about the fallacious 'security' they bring us.

'Who are arms under the authority of?' Politicians who, in the West, are elected and are obliged to justify their actions to their electors.

'Who do arms kill?' Workers, soldiers, future electors and fifty million starving people per year in the Third World, straight away. Arms kill only innocent people. Through our silence and our money we all support this butchery. Disarmament negotiations always take place at the highest level, never at the level of the 'consumers', and for good reason!

**GÉRARD.** — If we follow your reasoning, we should disarm all the western powers because, in our countries, we are free enough to risk our 'security', to give ourselves up without 'defence' to the countries who haven't got that liberty, and who do not intend to disarm . . .

**JEAN.** – Your objections would be justified if the countries of the Communist bloc were really independent of the techniques of the non-communist bloc, and if all these countries were inhabited by robots running on Stalinism. Western countries supply arms to China and computers to the Soviet Union. Don't have any illusions about it, gold doesn't smell the same as corpses. We still don't realize that all the armies in the world are made up of men, we only see rifles and equipment. All the powers that be, all the exploiters, take advantage of this blindness, and, as for us, we are afraid to open our eyes. We naively think that the Russians are afraid of our tanks and our bombs. Ridiculous. They are afraid of faith. They put Baptists, abstract painters and yogis in prison. They show the whole world where their fear, their weak point, is situated, where they see danger. And we don't understand!

**HILDEGARD.** — I would like to quote an extract from a letter that Monseignor Ménager, Archbishop of Reims and president of the French Committee for Justice and Peace, wrote to the Larzac farmers on the occasion of the harvest festival on the 22nd July 1974.[86]

'A country's collective security is an important question for us. You know that very well. But you bear witness to the fact that even the most sophisticated arms are not enough, and that the true force of resistance, if we are obliged to have recourse to it, resides in the soul of a people. The experience of non-violence, first of all prac-ticed instinctively, and then discovered systematically, points in that direction.'

Are we Christians going to remain blind? When it is a question of concrete dangers, of violence committed upon the whole of humanity, upon the body of Christ, are we going to come down on the side of the executioners because it is the safest way of saving our own skins? 'The spirit of truth, whom the world cannot receive, because it seeth him not, neither knoweth him; but you know him, for he dwelleth with you, and shall be in *you*' (John 14. 17).

**GÉRARD.** — We must listen to our generals. They know what our security is made of. For General Gallois, father of the French deterrent, the defence of our country ought to be in the hands of a regular army, the only sort that would be effective in a nuclear conflict.[87] It is all a matter of technique. Disarmament becomes a 'great hoax'[88] for the same general. The soul? The general's never heard of it!

In the constitution of Unesco it is written: 'Wars are born in men's spirits; the defences of peace should be developed in men's spirits.'

JEAN. — We pay taxes to pay for bombs and we want disarmament to cost nothing? To cost 'us' nothing? We put our defence into the hands of technicians and our security into the hands of politicians; we refuse to take our responsibilities. 'You only have to, you only have to . . .' Well, no.

In Britain, fifteen thousand employees of the aerospace branch of the Lucas Group drew up a plan with the help of their unions which would transform an industry oriented towards armaments into one which would be socially useful and economically profitable. The plan concerned the development of a vehicle which would be usable on the road and on the railway. It is going to be produced by the Centre for Alternative Industrial and Technological systems at North East London Polytechnic because the Lucas Group rejected it. This movement shows how technicians involved in the manufacture of arms became aware of their own human dignity, and as a result, of their responsibility as men.[89]

Politicians in all countries realize it: 'All plans have failed for fifty years, and yet disarmament concerns everyone.'[90] We should link learning about disarmament to learning about the rights of man; we should live disarmament, our disarmament, with love for the human being.

No country, no dictatorship ever attacks the United Nations. All dictatorships pour scorn on Amnesty International, that's obvious. If there had only been the U.N. Bokassa would still be killing children today. Non-violent movements work on non-violent civil defence, based on the responsibility of each individual, on the participation of all citizens. This defence is developed in a climate of respect and liberty, because the effectiveness of a defence lies not in technical prowess, but in conviction. The Americans were defeated in Indo-China, and 'Mr Klisko, a member of the Polish politburo, admitted that on their return from Czechoslovakia some soldiers had spread subversive ideas, and that, in the military district of Silesia alone, a hundred and fifty serving officers had had to be dismissed.'[91]

# VIII

HILDEGARD. — We can not take refuge in theories, nor shelter behind condemnations from bloc to bloc. Violence, arms are there, that's a fact; it's a massive, daily reality. The danger for us is habit, the acceptance of violence as a fatality. The danger for us is keeping quiet because we lack faith in our own effectiveness. We have no right to keep quiet, even if, for some people armaments are one of the demands of their faith, the safeguard of human and Christian values, and a rampart against unemployment.

In France, work on disarmament has been done by the M.A.N., the Arc community and by Reseau Espérance (Hope Network), as well as by other groups such as the International Fellowship of Reconciliation, and the M.D.P.L. (the Movement for Disarmament, Peace and Liberty). The action of Third World countries should bear a lot of weight in disarmament. The Third World countries are those who bear the brunt of our wrongdoing. Albert Tévoédjré[92] has suggested that 'some not very well-off countries decide, like Costa Rica, to do without national armed forces', and put themselves under the protection of the international community. In his opinion that would be the basis of a contract of solidarity which would really help the development of the countries concerned. Even if we stay within a purely 'military' context, a small developing country's army would be totally ineffective in a conflict on a world or continental scale. We must propose an 'international solidarity to the benefit of those nations who have had the strength to opt for general disarmament.'

There is no shortage of propositions, plans or opportunities for commitment. Non-violent proposals exist, and are lived out in all activities, both national and inter-national. No one can allow themselves to give up.

'I am not going to ask you to become saints (and yet that would be the solution), I am not going to say "Love each other!" (same comment). But only: "Replace the system that multiplies opportunities for hatred with another which favours and appeals to solidarity."[93] Now that change will not come to pass in society if it has not first come about in you. If you want to change the future, change yourselves.'

**GÉRARD.** — Of course, if I change, it is only a drop changing, and what about the ocean, what do you do with that? And if thousands of drops change, the ocean will still be the ocean, embracing everything, engulfing everything, including ridiculous little me. I shall be reduced to vapour before I see the wave coming to engulf me. And then 'change, change', all preachers can only say the same thing. Gérard, change into a choirboy, change into a progressive, into an anarchist, into . . .' I'm going to end up a cha-meleon or . . . change into Gérard, leave all the preachers standing there and go and live in my tent. 'Change yourself and the world will change!' I wonder if many men have tried. Look round you and see if the world has changed much. 'Change yourself', perhaps, yes, I agree, but how?

**JEAN.** — It's true, not many people have changed, have changed themselves. Alphonse Goettmann says we are 'amateur' Christians, otherwise the world would have caught fire ages ago, inflamed by our capacity for loving!

In life, we count on our biceps, our bank balance and our brains. It doesn't get us very far, even with official blessings on it. When we have finished taking stock of all that, what's left is discouragement, anxiety and fear. We find ourselves back once again on the path of violence, a very long way from the path of change. Change is adven-ture, it's going towards the unknown. I endanger my health with continual fasts and fatigue. I don't bother to earn my living like everybody else. I don't give a damn for diplomas, and why? For what result? Am I crazy, and Hildegard along with me? It's true! We talk of the Gospel everywhere, and the priests look at us askance! We're crazy! It's true. One day in Argentina I spoke to a Catholic government official about non-violence and he understood! Do you know what he did? He kicked me out straight away!

Hildegard was in South Africa, and when the government heard she was there, in no time at all she was arrested and interrogated. If I had to count on my own strength, on my own little brain, if I, Jean Goss, had to wait till all the great men and the less great approved of me, I would do better to go and buy a revolver.

That's what violence is all about; believing we are nothing more than sophisticated monkeys. But open your eyes. Were the men, the rare persons who have changed things in this world, who have brought a bit of happiness and love to this planet, were they heavyweights, athletes, bankers, Nobel Prizewinners in nuclear physics or professors of theology? No!

When things change in us they change at a completely different level. We are more than what we think and more than what we see. We are all made in the same style; we think that if we abandon our poor little certainties, our strength, our security and our learning, we will end up completely naked, even more incapable than when we were dressed. What happens is the opposite. That's the time things change in us and around us. It was when he had abandoned everything, that a force sprang up in Saint Francis and illuminated the world, and continues to do so.

We hang on to our inability to change the world because we hang on to our little ideas and our little desires. Our strength is not where we think it is.

**HILDEGARD.** — A lot of our western contemporaries have already joined Gérard in his tent. It's not worth the candle, is it? A lot of them are satisfied with the achievements of material progress and see in its pursuit the only goal of a possible 'change'. The reigning systems fill men's inner spaces with their trash, and oblige them to live in ever shallower levels of their own beings. Men become trunks, trees with neither roots nor branches. All certainties become truth. We paper over the cracks in social and capitalist progress in order to forget that we hunger for something else.

The Gospel, itself, has been reduced to a pious anthology which denies man any ability to change the world; that is reserved for God in heaven, and the human being is no more than a whipping-boy, begging a bad-tempered God to stop raining woes down on him. I understand men like Camus! 'Since the order of the world is regulated by death, perhaps it is better for God not to believe in him, and for us to fight against death with all our strength, without raising our eyes towards heaven where he remains silent.'[94]

**GÉRARD.** — I let myself go just now, I said everything that was in my heart because we must find out where the true source of non-violence lies, and what must be done to get past it. I know very well there are no recipes, and that all change is long and difficult. Can we afford to wait until we have all changed from little chrysalises into butterflies to save the world from being blown to pieces.

**JEAN.** — If you look no further than your own little heart you can't see the blood circulating. You don't even realize that at the bottom of your heart lies the force that every day enables you to break through the layers that paralyse you and reduce you to despair. Let yourself go into yourself, a bit further than you can see with your short-sighted eyes, and you will see. You mustn't tell Christians this, but that's what one calls praying. Unbelievers are afraid of the word, too, but it doesn't matter, as long as they find the treasure! The paths that lead to this treasure can lead through zen, yoga or asceticism; all these paths lead past that place in us where we are ourselves, wherein lies an energy which can surprise us, which surpasses our imagination. Change doesn't begin with each one of us. Believe me, it's been going on for some time. The light was not born yesterday and doesn't go out when you go to sleep.

**HILDEGARD.** — Men like Gandhi, Luthuli, King or Chavez had a decisive influence on non-violent struggles because of their own personal spiritual existence and the impact it had on others. They became spiritual and political guides. Their drive came from the depths of their own selves, and not from a philosophic or religious theory. Their deaths coincided with the decline of the struggles they had been involved in, which is particularly the case with the American and Indian non-violent movements. In my opinion, as far as non-violent struggles are concerned, the charismatic militant is given his ability to renew spiritual forces again and again, by taking them back to their roots and deepening them, not for himself personally but for the community. It is his duty to carry on the struggle with his gifts, but he should not bear the responsibility for the general plan. What happened in India and in the United States shows that it is politically dangerous to put the running of a movement into the hands of just a few people, however exceptional they may be, because they can easily be eliminated by the authorities, and because the groups at the grass-roots tend to hand over responsibility to them instead of taking it on themselves.

People sent by providence have a providential role to play, but no more, so it is essential for each one of us to set out on our own path instead of waiting for some hypothetical prophet to come along and act as our guide.

**JEAN.** — Each one of us can practise non-violence for a very simple reason: violence is everywhere, beginning with our own selves. If we wait to practise non-violence till the Russians or some other imagined enemy are in the streets, it will be too late. Every time another person crosses your path, whether for good or evil, you can have a non-violent encounter. Little by little this 'exercise' will sink into us and the change will take place. It's as sure as two and two make four.

Who has not experienced slander, mockery or cheating. Who is there among us who has not had to face these sorts of violence? There is no point in going on a non-violent demonstration if you have no practice in loving those who speak evil of you, if you don't face up to the person who tries to crush you under his dishonesty. Useless! Non-violence is a way of life, a continual exercise, and exercise is another word for commitment.

**HILDEGARD.** — In all honest banks throughout the world, money brings in interest. That's normal and automatic. If you perform a non-violent action, violence doesn't stop, it is not automatic, we don't 'draw' our interest. When the roots of non-violence do not go down to the depths, non-violent actions are tied to immediate success, and disappointments very soon get the better of strategic or tactical convictions.

'Some fell on stony places, where they had not much earth, and forthwith they sprung up, because they had no deepness of earth. And when the sun was up they were scorched; and because they had no root, they whithered away (Mt 13, 5–6).

**GÉRARD.** — Jewish wisdom says: 'He who wishes to bear the yoke of the Kingdom of heaven should first prepare his body.' Isn't this advice also advice for non-violent people?

**HILDEGARD.** — 'This is my body'; that's the testament of the pure non-violent one, Jesus. That's all we have to be non-violent with: a body; I have only that, I am only that. The body is not a way of being, it's the manifestation of *the* being.

**JEAN.** — The dead are no more violent than they are non-violent. For non-violence, you have got to be alive, I mean really alive, not just in physiological working order.

136

Non-violent people can be deaf, dumb, blind, old and crippled. I'll soon be seventy and no army in the world would take me as a recruit. Only the Lord has any use for me, with my poor old carcase going to pieces all over the place. That's because the Lord is not very fussy, but particularly because he doesn't act separately from us, he doesn't come along and add to what I do, what I live. The Lord lives what I live, so much so that I get the impression that he can't live without me. He is the life of my life, flesh of my flesh. I feel, no, I'm sure he says to us: 'I want you to be God with me, I wish you to be Myself. Have no fear, I'll pay for everything.' Yes, all that is so incredible that I understand atheists perfectly.

Sometimes friends reproach us with not giving any spiritual training on our tours. They are right. We come for scarcely a couple of hours, and then, off we go somewhere else. We only stay a short time with you. Our mission is to 'say'. Why shouldn't the word of the Lord go further and deeper than our poor language? Why shouldn't this same word contain your way, your truth and your life? That word will have His face for you, and I, in my poverty, I would only be able to veil it . . .

'And the word became flesh and dwelt among us.'

\* \* \*

In March 1973, I received a letter from my friend Alphonse Goettmann[95] inviting me to follow a non-violent training seminar given by someone called Jean Goss. The letter even talked about evangelical non-violence. A week later I got another letter from Alphonse Goettmann, thanking me for having enrolled. I was that much more surprised because I had thrown the first letter away without any afterthought. I didn't want to waste my time with evangelical dreamers! I had plenty of other things to do! My wife Madeleine was the one who had arranged it all. Since then she has always claimed she had asked my permission before enrolling us. I must confess there is a gap in my memory.

I must tell you more. Madeleine and I were married with a settlement based on the separate ownership of property — 'because of our professions,' said the solicitor. It is because of this contract (which I have never read) that I could tell her after the first half day of talks by Jean that I had no objection if she stayed, but that I, for my part, preferred to go home. I stayed. The second day the count-down to my own inner explosion approached zero. I stayed.

On the way back, on the motorway, I realized 'that this was what I was looking for'. The next day, and I repeat, the next day, our friends Anny and Joseph Schaefer, who had lived through those days with us, and we two, threw ourselves into our first non-violent action.

Dear reader, you understand why I dedicate this book to Madeleine first of all. And then I dedicate it to Alphonse Goettmann and Rachel his wife, because they were at the origin of so many upheavals in our life.

I also dedicate this book to Jean-François, Bruno and Marie-Odile, our children. Like their parents, they were not born non-violent. Our family is a 'manoeuvring range' for evangelical non-violence, I was going to say, for love. I think you understand me.

Gérard Houver

# Chronology

**Jean GOSS**

1912: Born in Lyon. Father: opera baritone and anarchist. Second child in a family of five.

1918: The family moves to Paris.

1924: Does various jobs: walk-on parts at the Châtelet theatre selling newspapers; trimmer in a printing works; apprentice binder.

1927: Printing worker, trade unionist.

1928: Works in a biscuit factory.

1937: Works for the railways at the Gare de Lyon: ticket office, bookings and information.

1939: Sergeant in the light artillery. Decorations: Croix de Guerre, Médaille Militaire.

1940: Prisoner in Germany.

1945: Liberation. Back to the railways.

1950: Meets Cardinal Ottaviani.

**Hildegard MAYR**

1930: Born in Vienna. Fourth child in a family of five. Father: Kaspar Mayr, co-founder of the International Fellowship of Reconciliation. Secondary school in Vienna. University in Vienna and Newhaven (USA): philosophy, philology and history.

1938 to 1945: Experience of persecution under Nazi regime.

1953:   General strike of railwaymen of which he is one of the leaders. Expelled from trade union for refusal to discontinue the strike. International meeting in Budapest.

1953:   PhD. Gold medal from Vienna university; Travelling secretary of International Fellowship of Reconciliation, priority East-West work.

1956:   Non-violent meeting in Warsaw.

1957:   Meeting in Moscow.

**1958:   Marriage.**

1958:   Work in Prague and Moscow. The first international meeting of the Catholic, Protestant and Orthodox churches on evangelical non-violence.

1959:   Work in Hungary, Poland, Czechoslovakia and the United States.

1960:   Birth of Myriam and Etienne.

1960:   Work in Rumania, Bulgaria and Yugoslavia.

1962:   Work in Latin America. Collaborated with the Vatican II Concile *Gaudium et Spes*, (caps. LXXVIII-LXXIX); meet Dom Helder Camara, Karl Rahner and Yves Congar, Bernhard Häring.

1963:   Work in Britain, Ireland, Scandinavia, Portugal and Spain.

1964–65:   Stay a year in Brazil with their twins Etienne and Myriam. The first non-violent groups in Latin America founded.

1966:   Montevideo, first international meeting on revolutionary non-violence (nineteen countries represented).

1967:   Brazil, first official national seminar on revolutionary non-violence.

1968:   Second theological conference of the Catholic, Protestant and Orthodox churches from the East and the West on evangelical non-violence at Vienna. Work with leading Latin American bishops including Dom Hildare Cômmand. Work in Prague. Dom Aloisio Lorscheider, Msgr. Proviño etc.

1970–71:   Stay a year with their children in Mexico. Work in Colombia, Venezuela, Chile, Argentina, the United States and Portugal.

1972:   Work in Spain, Portugal, Scandinavia and the Balkans.

1973:   Work in Angola, Mozambique and South Africa.

1974:   Work in Mozambique, Angola and Portugal. Second co-ordinating conference of Latin-American non-violent movements in Medellin (Colombia). Secretary: Adolfo Perez Esquivel, 1980 Nobel Peace Prize winner.

1974–5:   Work in Lebanon.

1976:   Work in Israel, South Africa, Rhodesia and Tanzania.

1978:   Bogota, seminar for bishops on the evangelical message of non-violent liberation.

1979:   Work in El Salvador; they are awarded the Prize and the Bruno-Kreisky Prize for their human rights work.

1980:   Work in Lebanon.

1981/82:   Work in Poland.

1983/85:   Work in the Philippines, Thailand and Bangladesh, Canada and USA.

1986:   Pax Christi USA award. Paul VI-teacher for Peace.

# *Notes*

## Chapter 1

1. *Panorama d'aujourd'hui*, February, 1981, no. 146, p. 31.
2. Sean MACBRIDE, *l'Exigence de la liberté*, Stock, Paris, 1981, p. 129.
3. Madeleine DELBREL, *Aujourd'hui la Bible*, XVI no. 231, Fayard, Mame Paris, 1970, p. 6.
4. René GIRARD, *La Violence et le Sacré*, Grasset, Paris, 1972, p. 208.
5. René GIRARD, *op. cit.*, p. 122.
6. René GIRARD, *op. cit.*, p. 30.
7. René GIRARD, *op. cit.*, p. 212.
8. Sean MACBRIDE, *op. cit.*, p. 234.
9. Jean TOULAT, 'Bombe N et Bombe M', *le Monde*, 26th February, 1981.
10. Jacques MONOD, *Le Hasard et la Nécessité*, Seuil, Paris, 1970, p. 188.
11. Alexander SOLZHENITSYN *Gulag Archipelago (l'Archipel de Goulag)*, Seuil, Paris, 1974, p. 128.

## Chapter 2

12. Martin Luther KING, *la Force d' aimer*, Casterman, Paris, 1964, p. 73.
13. Corretta KING, *Ma vie avec Martin Luther King*, Stock, Paris, 1969, p. 160.
14. René GIRARD, *Des choses cachées depuis la fondation du monde* Grasset, Paris, 1978, p. 207.
15. René GIRARD, *Des choses cachées . . .*, *op. cit.*, p. 208.
16. René GIRARD, *op. cit.*, p. 237.
17. FORESTI, *Violence ou non-violence*, Collection Nouvelle Cité, Paris, 1971, p. 75.

18. Gilles SENGES, 'La pasionaria irlandaise de la paix', *le pelerin*, March, 1981, no. 5129, pp. 47–8.
19. Extracts from *Walesa*, by François GAULT, Le Centurion, Paris, pp. 29–31.
20. Alexander SOLZHENITSYN, *The Decline of Courage*, Seuil, Paris, 1978, p. 38.

## Chapter 3

21. René GIRARD, *Des choses cachées . . .*, *op. cit.*, p. 208.
22. Jacques, ELLUL, Politique de Dieu et politique de l'homme, Edations universitaires, Paris, 1966, p. 164.
23. Meister ECKHART, quoted from memory.
24. Paul FOULQUE, 'Sentiments, passions et Signes', Alain, quoted in *Psychologie*, Editions de l'Ecole, 1947, p. 641.
25. Thomas MERTON, *Zen and the Birds of Appetite*, New Directions, 1968, pp. 123–124.
26. Suzanne LASSIER, Gandhi et la non-violence, Seuil, Paris, 1970, p. 138.
27. Paul TILLICH, *The Courage to Be*, Fontana Library, 1962, p. 57.
28. Karlfried Graf DURKHEIM. *Hara. centre vital de l'homme*, le courrier du livre, Paris, 1971, p. 67.
29. News Bulletin of the episcopal conference in Paraguay, no. 26, September, 1972.
30. Suzanna LASSIER, *op. cit.*, p. 134.

## Chapter 4

31. René GIRARD, *Des Choses Cachées . . .*, *op. cit.*, p. 165.
32. Jean SULIVAN, *Exode*, 'Connivence', Desclée de Brouwer, Paris, 1980, p. 145.
33. Antonio FRAGOSO, *Evangile et Révolution Sociale.*, Cerf, Paris, 1969, pp. 132–133.
34. Saint Francis of Assisi, *Decherance*, Plon, Paris, 1885, p. XV.
35. Saint Francis of Assisi, *op. cit.*, p. XII.
36. James MAYER, O.F.M., *Die Sozialen Ideale des Hl Franziskus von Assisi*, Drittordenszentrale, Schwyz, 1943, p. 35.

37. J. K. Nyerere, *The Basis of African Socialism*, Ujamaa, 1962, quoted in Alternatives non-violentes, no. 9–10, 1975.
38. G. KERNIEZ, *Karma Yoga*, Tallandier, Paris, 1973, p. 183.
39. Quoted from *Encyclopedia Universalis*, Paris; p. 870.
40. Jean SULIVAN, *Exode*, 'Connivence' Desclée de Brouwer, Paris, 1980, p. 145.

Chapter 5

41. Jacques LEAUTE, *Notre violence*, Denoel, Paris, 1977, quoted in Encyclopaedia Universalis, Paris, 1972, p. 495.
42. Barthélemy de LIGT, *Contre toute guerre*, Pensée et Action, Bruxelles, 1943.
43. G. PEYTAN DE FAUGERES, *La Modernité de Machiavel*, Mercure de France, 1932, p. 513.
44. B. de LIGT, *Pour vaincre sans violence*, Mignolet et Storz, Paris, 1935, pp. 17–19.
45. Suzanne LASSIER, *op. cit.*, p. 149.
46. Alain PEYREFITTE, *Quand la Chine s'éveillera*, Fayard, Paris, 1973, p. 372.
47. John-Paul II, *France, que fais tue de ton baptême?*, Le Centurion, 1980, Paris, p. 223.
48. John-Paul II, *op. cit.*, p. 104.
49. John-Paul II, *op. cit.*, p. 105.
50. James McNEISH, *le Combat de Danilo Dolci*, Stock, Paris, 1965, p. 123.
51. Non-violent union leader of Mexican farm-workers in the USA.
52. Joël de ROSNAY, 'Joël de Rosnay s'explique', *Lire*, Paris, January 1980, p. 31.
53. Jean SULIVAN, *op. cit.*, p. 169.
54. Quoted from a lecture by Mgr Germain de Saint-Denis.

Chapter 6

55. Jacques RUFFIE, 'De la biolgie à la culture' *Lire*, Paris, October, 1977, p. 169.
56. Claude CHARMES, Promovère, no. 17, March 1979.
57. Jacques LEAUTE, *op. cit.* from *Encyclopaedia Universalis*, 1978, p. 495.

58. Final document of the 1977 International Meeting of Latin American bishops, quoted by Hildegard GOSS in *l'Homme face à l'injustice*, Austrian Social Academy, Europaverlag, Vienna.

59. Lluis Mario XIRINACS, *La Sentinelle de la Liberté*, Editions ouvières, Paris, 1977, p. 196.

60. Bernard CHEVALIER, *l'Abbè Pierre, Emaüs ou venger l'homme*, Le Centurion, Paris, 1980, p. 222.

61. Albert TÉVOÉDJRÉ, *Pauvreté et richesse des peuples*, Editions ouvrières, Paris, 1978, p. 169.

62. The word 'utopia' was invented by Thomas More in 1516. It was the title of a book describing life in an imaginary country. A utopia is a prototype, a model which enables us to imagine new solutions to problems. Thomas More imagined free medical care for the sick and the aged, completely free education at all levels: 'Each man works six hours a day at the trade which is best suited to his ability. There are no latches on the doors of the houses. In fact everything is held in common among the citizens. With gold, the citizens make chamber pots.' (A. PREVOST, *Thomas More et la crise de la pensée européenne*, Mame, p. 104.)

On the 6th July 1535, Thomas More died on the scaffold because he was a 'consciencious objector'. He refused to bow down before the authority of his king, Henry VIII. 'I see no authority which has the right to force someone to change their mind and make his conscience pass from one side to another. For I alone bear the responsibility for my soul.' (letter to his daughter)

63. Albert TÉVOÉDURÉ, *op. cit.*, see footnote 62.

64. Julien FREUND, 'Violence, signe de notre temps', *Cahiers universitaires catholiques*, Paris, no. 3, 1980–81.

65. Raoul SALAN, 'En Algérie, la torture', *Historama*, no. 260, Paris, July 1973, p. 48.

66. Bernard CHEVALIER, *op. cit.*, p. 125.

67. *Panorama d'aujourd'hui*, February, 1981, no. 146, Paris, p. 32.

68. The Orthodox theologian Olivier Clément writes that 'The Church has no need to impose its methods, whether they be non-violent or not. It must bear witness at all times to the creative power of love. The problem then is not one of violence or non-violence; its solution, always incomplete, is

the ability to metamorphose, as much as possible, in each historical circumstance, destructive violence into creative strength.' (Olivier CLEMENT, *Questions sur l'homme*, Stock, 1972, p. 139.)

For this writer non-violence is just a 'system' based on 'resignation' and 'weakness', and it is *understandable* that he cannot accept it. We just have to ask how a Church can authentically bear witness to the creative power of love to find the meaning of non-violence.

69. Gaston BOUTHOUL, *Avoir la Paix*, Grasset, Paris, 1967, p. 62.
70. *Paris-Match*, 27 February, 1981, p. 76.
71. Jean-Jacques SERVAN-SCHREIBER, *Le Défi mondial*, Fayard, Paris, 1980, p. 276.
72. *Gardarem lo Larzac*, supplement no. 1, June, 1975.

**Chapter 7**

73. Martin Luther KING, *Revolution non-violente*, Payot, Paris, 1965, p. 104.
74. Bernard CHARBONNEAU, *Je fus*, Charbonneau, 1980, p. 225.
75. Suzanne LASSIER, *op. cit.*, p. 159.
76. Bernard CHARBONNEAU, *op. cit.*, p. 215.
77. Albert TÉVOÉDJRÉ, *op. cit.*, p. 15.
78. *Le Monde* 27/28 May 1979, interview with René Girard.
79. Jeanne ANCELET-HUSTACHE, *Maître Eckhart et la mystique rhénane*, Coll. 'Maîtres spirituelles', Seuil, Paris, 1971.
80. In recent years the Fellowship (IFOR), on the international level, has started to refer once again to spiritual motivations in its action in favour of the absolute respect of the human being. In 1977 Hildegard and Jean resumed leadership roles in IFOR. In 1988, at the IFOR Council in Assisi, they were elected IFOR's Honourary Presidents.
81. Alternatives non-violentes, April, 1976, nos. 15–16, p. 120.
82. René DOUMERC, *Dialogues avec Lanza del Vasto*, Cerf, Paris, 1981, p. 220.
83. René DOUMERC, *op. cit.*, p. 48.
84. Sean MACBRIDE, *op. cit.*, p. 233.
85. *Id*, p. 232.

86. *Larzac Informations: Special Tiers Monde*, 22nd July, 1979.
87. Pierre-Marie GALLOIS, *L'Adieu aux armées'*, Albin Michel, Paris, 1977.
88. Pierre-Marie GALLOIS, *La Grande Berne* (The great hoax), Plon, Paris, 1975.
89. *Temoignage chrétien*, 1st March, 1981, no. 1911.
90. M. TAITTINGER, *La Vie*, May, 1978, no. 1708.
91. *Alternatives non-violentes*, April, 1976, nos. 15–16.


Chapter 8

92. Albert TÉVOÉDJRÉ, *op. cit.*, p. 169.
93. Albert TÉVOÉDJRÉ, *op. cit.*, p. 186 (quotation from Denis de Rougement).
94. Albert CAMUS, *La Peste*, la Pléiade, Gallimard, Paris, 1962, p. 1321.
95. Orthodox priest and founder of a Center of Metitation near Metz, France.

# I STEP, I MOUNT: THE VISION OF JOHN HENRY NEWMAN

*Edited by Robert Van de Weyer and Pat Saunders*

In this selection of extracts, with an extended biographical introduction, we look at the life, ideas and poetry of Cardinal Newman. An Anglican for the first half of his life, Newman became the spiritual leader of the Oxford Movement, seeking sacramental renewal in the Anglican Church. In 1845, he became a Roman Catholic and set out to raise the importance of the laity in the eyes of that church.

# THE SPIRITUAL KISS: THE VISION OF SAINT AELRED OF RIEVAULX

*Edited by Robert Van de Weyer and Pat Saunders*

In this third volume in the Vision of . . . series, the life of Aelred, the official biographer of Edward the Confessor, is considered in the light of his writing. He was a writer in the mystical tradition, severe in his interpretation of the monastic rule but with a genius for friendship. The 'spiritual kiss' to which the title refers is given 'not by the touch of the mouth but by the affection of the heart'.

# HIDDEN HEROES OF THE GOSPELS
## Feminine Counterparts of Jesus

*Joseph A. Grassi*

In this fascinating new book, Joseph Grassi studies the Gospels as narrative drama, and discovers that the ideal disciple is often portrayed as a woman. Pursuing a detailed analysis of the literary structure of each of the four Gospels, Grassi shows how the text works to point out the model forms of discipleship, and how women fit this model. Among the women portrayed are the poor widow in the Temple, the daughter of Jairus, the Syro-Phoenician woman, and Mary Magdalene. £4.99